COLLINS

OILS

WORKSHOP

OILS
WORKSHOP

A PRACTICAL COURSE
IN OIL PAINTING TO DEVELOP
SKILLS AND CONFIDENCE

Richard Pikesley

HarperCollins*Publishers*

ACKNOWLEDGEMENTS

I should like to thank all those who have given their time and talent so generously to the making of this book.

Special thanks are due to all the artists for saying 'yes' and sending lovely pictures, and to Caroline Churton of HarperCollins, Caroline Hill and Angela Gair, who helped to turn all the raw ideas and images into a book.

*All paintings are by Richard Pikesley
unless stated otherwise.*

PAGE 1:
Richard Pikesley,
*Crowds on
Weymouth
Promenade,*
30.5 x 35.5 cm
(12 x 14 in)

PAGE 2:
Richard Pikesley,
Café at Villandry,
60.5 x 50.5 cm
(24 x 20 in)

First published in 1997
by HarperCollins*Publishers*, London

© Richard Pikesley, 1997

Richard Pikesley asserts the moral right to be identified
as the author of this work.

A catalogue record for this book is available from the British Library

*Editor: Angela Gair
Design and Typesetting: Caroline Hill
Photographer: Jon Bouchier*

ISBN 0 00 412964 4

Set in Palatino and Futura
Colour origination in Singapore, by Colourscan
Produced by HarperCollins Hong Kong

CONTENTS

ABOUT THIS BOOK

The aim of this book is to encourage you to learn by doing, just as you would in a practical painting workshop led by a tutor. Along with instructional teaching and general guidelines in the text, you will find practical exercises and projects for you to do, designed to help you to develop as an artist. As you practise and become more visually receptive and perceptive about the world around you, your own ideas, and personal style, will begin to emerge.

Most of the chapters contain one main project and, in some cases, a number of exercises. If you carry out all of these before moving on, they will effectively help you to understand and practise the teaching.

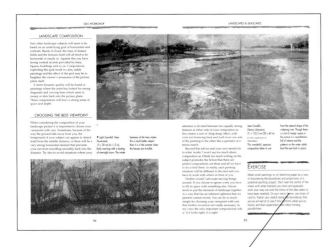

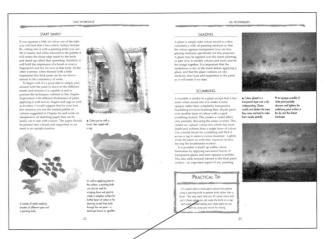

EXERCISES

These are designed to complement the teaching contained in each chapter. Some of the exercises are quite short and should not take too long to do; others may require a little more time. Their aim is to get you painting and thinking for yourself.

PRACTICAL TIPS

Throughout the book you'll also come across practical tips. These highlight some useful hints about working methods and provide a few solutions to everyday painting problems.

SELF-ASSESSMENTS

At the end of each project, you'll find a number of self-assessment questions relating to the work you have just completed; these are intended to draw your attention to particular aspects of your painting, in the same way that a professional tutor might help you to assess your work in a practical workshop.

PROJECTS

The projects, of varying degrees of difficulty, concentrate on more specific aspects of painting, with a view to sparking off ideas which you can then try to interpret in your own way.

You should take your time with the projects and be prepared to reread relevant sections of the text as often as you need to enable you to tackle them successfully. After all, there are no short cuts to learning to paint well!

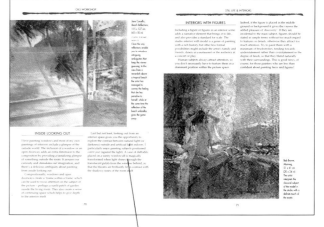

DEMONSTRATIONS

Because you can learn a great deal by watching professional artists at work, several demonstration paintings by the author are included in the book. These show how a painting is developed from the initial drawing to the finished work, and you are taken step-by-step through each stage so that you will understand

what techniques are used and can see how particular effects are created.

IDEAS & INSPIRATION

The paintings in the book, by the author and other well-known contemporary artists, cover a wide range of different subject matter. Some of these paintings are meant to complement and clarify points explained in the text, but others are included to show how style and technique vary from one artist to another,

emphasizing the importance of being original in your creative work. They can help you to extend your attitudes and horizons – and fire your enthusiasm. They are there for you to enjoy!

CHAPTER ONE

THE MEDIUM OF OILS

Of the many people who take up painting each year, comparatively few choose to tackle oil painting straight away. It is often considered 'difficult' compared with other media, perhaps something to be tried later. Yet oil paint can be the perfect vehicle for anyone learning to paint. To begin with, oil paint has a sensuous, tactile quality that makes it very pleasurable to use. It also has a versatility no other medium can match, and its naturally slow way of drying means that, unlike acrylics, gouache and watercolour, it can be extensively manipulated on the painting surface. This allows you more time for reflection and adjustment – you can think about drawing and composition, tone and colour without the pressure of getting the painting right first time. It also gives you the opportunity to experiment with paint, knowing that if something doesn't work it can be scraped down and a fresh start made.

▶ *Sundial Trees,*
76 x 61cm
(30 x 24 in)

Pink Deckchair,
Lyme Regis,
20 x 25 cm
(8 x10 in)

8

DEVELOPMENT OF OIL PAINTS

Before the invention of oil paint in the fifteenth century, artists painted with egg tempera, which consisted of colour pigments ground into egg yolk. When applied to absorbent gesso panels the paint dried almost instantly, thus demanding a meticulous approach in which the image was developed from a network of tiny cross-hatched brushstrokes. By using oil as a binder instead of egg yolk, the paint was rendered more brushable and slower-drying and the colours richer and more translucent. This allowed artists to work with greater

Ken Howard,
The Venetian Model,
102 x 122 cm (40 x 48 in)

COURTESY OF MANYA IGEL FINE
ARTS LTD

Michaelmas,
25 x 20 cm (10 x 8 in)

freedom, applying colours in broad areas and softening brushstrokes to create seamless passages of colour and tone.

Before the industrial age made tube colours a commonplace, artists had to prepare their own paints. A painter's studio was very much a workshop, where pigments had to be ground by hand into a fine powder and blended with oils and resins in just the right proportions. As the paints could not be stored for any length of time they had to be made up in small batches, just enough for the next day's work. This also meant that painting was largely a studio-based activity as the paints could not be transported outside.

With the introduction of collapsible tin tubes of oil paint and lightweight canvases in the mid-nineteenth century, the artist's studio was suddenly portable. Artists could now work directly from nature, and the move towards painting in the open air was born.

OIL PAINTING TODAY

The easy availability of high-quality oil paints and mediums today means that a degree in alchemy is no longer a necessary prerequisite to painting in oils, though a basic knowledge of the physical properties of your materials is always helpful. The following chapters aim to get you painting confidently as you begin to explore oil paints for yourself.

CHAPTER TWO

MATERIALS & EQUIPMENT

There is a common misconception that oil painting is complicated, and one of my aims in this book is to show that it is actually a straightforward process as long as you keep your materials simple and ensure that they are compatible with each other. I would always argue for a small range of good-quality materials chosen to work well together, rather than buying up everything in the shop.

There is no need to encumber yourself with masses of equipment to paint successfully in oils. On many of my painting trips abroad I limit myself to what can be carried on the back of a bicycle. A few boards, a handful of oil colours, a couple of brushes and a bottle of thinning medium are all that I require. I carry everything in a pochade box – a wooden box with a slide-out palette and a lid which acts as an easel.

Fred Dubery, *Worktable*, 23 x 27cm (9 x 10½ in). A ready-made subject found in a corner of the artist's studio demonstrates that a good working environment can also be a spur to your most personal work. As well as having a poetic quality, this little painting is a marvellous essay in handling tones and depicting the subtle nuances of colour on white surfaces.

A selection of brushes; a painting knife; parchment and wooden palettes; artists' oil colours; turpentine and painting medium. The requirements for oil painting are surprisingly few.

PAINTS

Oil paints are sold in tubes of varying size and are available in two grades, usually known as Artists' (first grade) and Students' (second grade) colours. If you can afford to do so, use Artists' colours; they are rather more expensive but the quality is superb. To lower the price, Students' colours are sometimes made with substitute pigments and also include fillers and extenders to bulk them up. This produces paints that lack a little of the brilliance of the more expensive range but which are more uniform in their handling qualities.

Artists' quality colours are priced in bands according to the cost of the pigment and you may find that one manufacturer classifies a particular colour in a lower band than another, thus lowering the cost.

COLOURS

You will find more about choosing colours in Chapter Six, but with the following 12 colours you will be able to do everything covered by this book and have a good working palette as a basis for further experiment.

Titanium White
Lemon Yellow
Cadmium Yellow Deep
Raw Sienna
Venetian Red
Cadmium Scarlet
Permanent Rose
French Ultramarine
Cerulean Blue
Opaque Chrome Oxide Green
Terre Verte
Raw Umber

BRUSHES

Brushes for oil painting come in a dauntingly wide range of shapes, sizes and materials. You don't need a huge variety, but it pays to buy good-quality brushes as they last longer and hold their shape better.

The traditional material for oil-painting brushes is hog bristle. Tough and hard-wearing, bristle brushes hold a lot of paint and are designed to withstand being worked against the textured surface of canvas.

I find it useful to have a few small soft-hair brushes for delicate linear work. Sables are very expensive, but there are now some excellent synthetic soft-hair brushes on the market, and also mixtures of sable and synthetic.

Each brush shape makes a different kind of mark, but some are more versatile than others. Rounds are good general-purpose brushes; use the body of the brush for laying in broad areas of colour and the tip for fine details. Flats are square-ended brushes that can be used flat, for broad areas, or on edge for fine lines. A word of caution, however; flats make a very distinctive square-edged mark that can be a little too assertive when used to the exclusion of other types of brush. Brights have shorter bristles than flats and produce strongly textured strokes. Filberts are similar to flats but have slightly rounded ends that make soft, tapered strokes.

Every brush will put the paint down in a slightly different way and will to some extent determine the character of the finished painting, but swopping about too much between lots of brushes can make the painting look fussy. You can make surprisingly delicate marks with a large brush, and remember you can always cut in with the background colour if a brushstroke spreads too far. In fact, it is this overlapping of strokes to revise edges that gives oil painting much of its character.

PALETTES

Oil-painting palettes come in many shapes and sizes and which one you choose will depend a lot on how you work. Disposable parchment palettes come in pads with tear-off sheets and are convenient if you don't like the chore of cleaning up. On windy days they can be a little difficult to keep under control and they seem to be available only in rather small sizes. My preference is for a large kidney-shaped

My old palette laid out with oil colours and ready for work.

mahogany palette. These balance well on your arm if you have to stand at the easel for a long time, and they hold plenty of paint. Dark toned wooden palettes are rather better than white melamine ones as it is much easier to make tone and colour judgments against the darker surface. Mahogany is expensive but a sheet of good-quality ply, cut and shaped to your preferred style, is just as good.

A new wooden palette will improve greatly with age and as it absorbs linseed oil from the paints. If you do make your own, it is a good idea to rub raw linseed oil into it every time you clean it, or whenever it begins to look starved. Not only will your palette become a more beautiful object, but it will absorb less oil from your paints and thus keep them workable for a good deal longer.

If you are working in the studio and don't have to carry the palette, a large sheet of plate glass is very good as this can be rested on a table with sheets of coloured paper slipped underneath. As the painting progresses the colour and tone of the paper can be changed to give a similar context for the colour mixing as is found in the painting.

SOLVENTS AND MEDIUMS

Oil paint generally needs to be thinned to a workable consistency by adding either a solvent

A variety of oil-painting supports, including raw canvas and wooden stretchers, assembled canvases, prepared boards and oil sketching paper.

or a medium (a mixture of solvent and oil). In the initial stages of a painting, a solvent such as distilled turpentine or white spirit is all that is required. If you find the smell of turpentine unpleasant or it gives you a headache, try one of the low-odour alternatives available from artists' suppliers.

The most commonly used painting medium is a mixture of linseed oil and turpentine. Linseed oil dries to a glossy finish, but it does tend to yellow with age, so look for a proprietary oil-painting medium as this contains a smaller proportion of linseed oil

As the painting progresses you should gradually increase the percentage of oil added to the paint in order to prevent cracking of the paint surface (this process is known as painting 'fat over lean' – more on this in Chapter Three).

OTHER EQUIPMENT

To move paint about on the palette you'll need a palette knife. The type sold as painting knives, with a cranked shaft and a flexible steel blade, are easier to use than the straight type and will help prevent getting paint on your knuckles. A clip-on dipper with two wells will fix onto the side of the palette to carry solvent and medium. A selection of cans and jars is useful for washing brushes, together with a supply of lint-free rags or kitchen towel.

SUPPORTS
The word 'support' simply means the surface on which you paint. Canvas has been the preferred choice of oil painters for centuries because the springiness of the taut cloth gives it a working

◀ **1** The stretcher bars are morticed and can be pushed together by hand or gently tapped together using a hammer and a block of wood. You will need two matching pairs of stretcher bars.

character quite unlike anything else. Stretched canvas comes into its own when making large paintings and its light weight means that it is easy to transport. On the negative side, paintings on canvas are easily dented if not handled and stored with care.

You can buy canvas ready-stretched and primed on a wooden stretcher frame, or, more economically, by the metre from a roll so that you can stretch it yourself. You can buy wooden stretcher bars in a variety of lengths and assemble them into any shape or size you like, whereas pre-stretched canvases come in a limited range.

Linen canvas is the most costly, but it is the best quality. A medium weight cotton duck is cheaper, and perfectly adequate. Both are available primed or unprimed, but to begin with I should choose a primed one. Although a little more expensive, it will save you having to do this yourself. You may also be offered a choice of oil-primed or acrylic-primed canvas. My preference would be for oil-primed, but if you choose this remember that you cannot apply acrylic paint on it as you can with the acrylic-primed version because the oil in the primer repels acrylics, and the paint eventually comes away from the support.

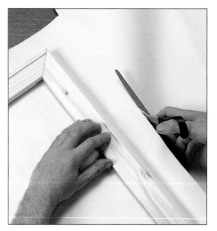

▲ **2**

▲ **3**

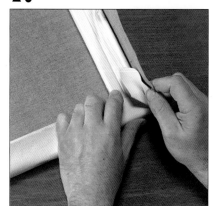

▲ **4**

▲ **5**

2 Cut a piece of canvas, allowing a 5cm (2in) overlap all round the stretcher.

3 Lay the stretcher bevel-side down on the canvas. Fold the canvas round to the back and secure with a staple at the centre of one of the long stretcher bars. Pull the canvas as tight as you can and drive a staple into the centre of the opposite side. Repeat the procedure for the remaining two sides, then drive in more staples at 5cm (2in) intervals.

4 Make a neat fold at each corner and secure with staples fired into the back of the stretcher bar. Do not staple across the mitre join, as this will make it impossible to tighten the canvas later on.

5 Driving a pair of wedges into each corner will force the sides apart and tighten the canvas.

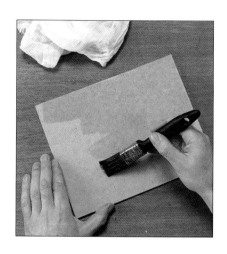

◀ **1** Heat up a solution of rabbit-skin glue in a double boiler (about 30g of glue to 500ml of water). When this is warm and fluid, paint it onto the smooth surface of a hardboard panel.

▲ **2**

▲ **3**

▲ **4**

▲ **5**

2 Cut a piece of muslin to size, allowing a 5cm (2in) overlap all round. Press the fabric into the wet glue and smooth it tight across the surface.

3 Apply another layer of glue over the muslin, brushing from the centre outwards and smoothing out any creases.

4 Trim the corners with scissors.

5 Turn the board over and stick down the surplus edges of the cloth. Leave to dry flat overnight before priming with an oil, not acrylic, primer. If you prefer a less textured surface, apply two or three layers of primer, sanding lightly between layers.

BOARDS AND PANELS

Hardboard, which you can buy from builders' suppliers, is an excellent yet inexpensive support for oils. Most artists use the smooth side, as the rough side has a very insistent, mechanical texture. Plywood and MDF (medium-density fibreboard) are also suitable for oil painting. Prepare the board with primer if you like a white surface, or, if you prefer to work on a neutral mid-toned surface, simply apply a coat of glue size or PVA.

You can buy commercially prepared canvas boards, which are relatively inexpensive and are ideal when trying out oils for the first time. However, the cheaper ones have a rather slippery surface that some artists find difficult to work on.

I prefer to prepare my own panels by covering them with a layer of muslin. My method is outlined in the photographic sequence. It may seem a bit fiddly at first, but once you are producing paintings regularly it is good to have more control of your materials. I like to prepare my panels so that the grain of the muslin is very nearly obscured by the primer, which is then sanded fairly smooth. Beginners are sometimes puzzled about why paint handling can seem rather unpredictable at times. It doesn't often occur to them how much influence the surface qualities of their canvas or board have. Find out what suits you and then select or prepare your surfaces accordingly.

PAPER

Paper makes a very good support for oil paint providing it is well prepared. The easiest option is to buy oil sketching paper, available either in loose sheets or pads. The paper has a sympathetic matt surface and, providing very thick impasto is avoided, its flexibility shouldn't be a problem. The big advantage of paper is that you can easily adjust its proportions to fit a particular composition. Paintings made on paper should be framed under glass.

EASELS

Some sort of easel is a must, as you need to be able to stand back from your work from time to time. I have a large radial easel for studio use and a lightweight portable one with a built-in paint box for painting out of doors. If you can only afford one easel I would recommend a lightweight sketching easel, made of either beechwood or alloy, as the most versatile. It will carry a canvas up to a metre or so high, is

◀ The author working in his studio. A well-organized space in which to work is a great help, although the basic requirements for oil painting are simple and few.

portable and can be folded away when not in use. There are some very good box easels on the market that combine an easel with a box for all your kit, a palette and a way of carrying spare canvases and wet paintings.

Standing to paint at a radial easel. Try to work in a good light and with space behind you so you can step back to assess your work.

A STUDIO AT HOME

As you've seen, your painting equipment won't necessarily take up a lot of space. A few colours, a canvas or board, solvents and brushes and a sketching easel are all you need to paint on a smallish scale. A spare room can easily be used as a studio and everything can be stored in a cupboard when the space is needed for other things. If you are painting in a room sometimes used for other activities, using a low-odour solvent and disposable parchment palettes will make your painting easier to live with.

CHAPTER THREE

OIL TECHNIQUES

Oil paint can be used in many different ways and indeed the sheer versatility of the medium can be a little daunting at first because it seems to offer you more choices at every turn. To begin with, the colours may be used thickly to build up a rich impasto that retains the marks and ridges left by the brush. Or they can be diluted to a delicate, wash-like consistency. Between these two extremes tremendous variation is possible and part of the delight of using oil colours is that these different densities of paint can be juxtaposed and contrasted in the same painting, thus adding to the expressive and textural qualities of the finished image.

Oil paints can be used for making rapid little sketches or for huge, ambitious canvases that may take months to complete. Unlike watercolours and acrylics, oil paint dries at a steady, predictable pace and remains workable while it's wet. This means you won't be hanging around on a damp day waiting for the paint to dry, or fighting against it drying too quickly on a hot day.

After many years of daily use, I still find oil paint to be exciting stuff and I enjoy it for its tactile quality and marvellous expressive range. I even love the smell of it!

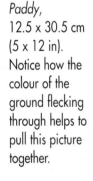

Paddy,
12.5 x 30.5 cm
(5 x 12 in).
Notice how the colour of the ground flecking through helps to pull this picture together.

▶ *Daffodils and Willow Wands*, 61 x 50 cm (24 x 19¾ in). This painting was completed in three sessions over a period of several weeks, so the flowers and the willow catkins had to be replaced several times. Although some areas of the painting are many layers thick, in other parts the ground can be clearly seen.

START SIMPLY

If you squeeze a little oil colour out of the tube you will find that it has a thick, buttery texture. By cutting into it with a painting knife you can lift it cleanly and when returned to the palette it will retain the sharp edge made by the knife and stand up rather than spreading. Similarly it will hold the impression of a brush or even a fingerprint and dry for ever in that form. At the other extreme, when thinned with a little turpentine this thick paste can be run down almost to the consistency of water.

To begin with it's a good idea to simply play around with the paint to discover the different marks and textures it is capable of and to practise the techniques outlined in this chapter. Experiment with different thicknesses of paint, applying it with knives, fingers and rags as well as brushes. I would suggest that for your first few sessions you use the limited palette of colours suggested in Chapter Six and work on inexpensive oil sketching paper that can be easily cut to size with scissors. The paper should be pinned onto a board and supported on an easel in an upright position.

▲ Colour put on with a brush, then wiped with a rag.

A variety of marks made by brushes of different types and a painting knife.

As well as applying paint to the surface, a painting knife can also be used for scraping down wet paint to create a receptive surface for further layers of colour or for drawing incised lines back through the wet paint – a technique known as *sgrafitto*.

GLAZING

A glaze is simply tube colour mixed to a thin consistency with oil-painting medium so that the colour appears transparent (you can buy glazing mediums specifically for this purpose). A glaze may be applied over the entire painting, or part of it, to modify colours and tones and tie the image together. It is important that the underlayer is dry to the touch before applying a glaze, and that the glaze contains an oily medium; don't just add turpentine to the paint as it will make it too lean.

SCUMBLING

A scumble is similar to a glaze except that it has some white mixed into it to make it semi-opaque rather than completely transparent. Scumbling involves brushing thin, dryish paint over another layer of colour with a rapid scrubbing motion. This creates a veiled effect, only partially obscuring the areas covered. This creates an 'optical' colour mix which has more depth and richness than a single layer of colour. Use a bristle brush for scumbling and flick it across a rag to remove excess moisture. Lightly scrub the paint on with free, vigorous strokes, leaving the brushmarks evident.

It is possible to build up subtle colour harmonies by applying successive layers of transparent glazes and semi-opaque scumbles. This also adds textural interest to the final paint surface – an important aspect of any painting.

▲ Colour glazed in a transparent layer over a dry underpainting. Glazes modify and darken the areas they cover and tend to make them recede spatially.

▼ An opaque scumble of white paint partially obscures and lightens the underlying paint surface in the sky and the distant landscape.

PRACTICAL TIP

It's a good idea to move paint around the palette using a painting knife or palette knife rather than a brush. That way, each time you lift some colour and put it down again you can wipe the knife on a rag and avoid contaminating your clean paint as you might by using your brush for mixing.

Marans Cockerel,
19 x 20 cm (7½ x 8 in).
This little study had to be
painted quickly and the
warm orange-red of the dry
imprimatura helped to
establish the tones as well as
unifying the image.
Opportunistic painting like
this demands good
preparation beforehand.

TINTING THE GROUND

You can paint directly onto a white ground, but
many artists prefer to tint the ground first with
a thin wash of colour. This is known as an
imprimatura, and its purpose is to provide a
neutral mid-tone against which it is easier to
judge the lights and darks. It also tones down
the glaring white of the canvas and helps to
tie the painting together in the later stages.

The colour chosen for the *imprimatura* is often
a neutral grey or earth colour, which provides
a subtle mid tone. Alternatively, you could
choose something which is the complementary
(opposite) of the dominant colour in the

Painted quickly into a wet wash, this little study of bottles shows the juicy quality of paint handled in this way. Remember, though, that a lot will depend on the delicacy with which you place the paint onto the wet underlayer.

composition. An earthy red ground will give added brilliance to a predominantly green landscape, for example. A harmonizing ground also works well; try using blue-grey for a seascape, or pink for a sunset.

Dilute the paint with a little turpentine and brush it loosely over the canvas or board, or wipe it on with a rag. This veil of colour should be very thin so that it dries quickly and subsequent layers of paint bond well with the support. Leave the *imprimatura* to dry for at least a day before you start painting. For practical reasons I tend to tint my canvases and boards in batches with a variety of colours to suit different subjects.

WORKING INTO A WET WASH

An alternative way of working is to paint straight into a wash of colour while it is still wet. This produces a very fluid, juicy sort of paint handling right from the start, but it can be a little less controllable. One advantage of this method is that if you want a particular passage to be very luminous and intense you can wipe back to the white of the ground and apply the colour in the form of a transparent wash over the white ground. Wet-in-wet is a feature of *alla-prima* painting, where each stroke is painted next to or over another wet stroke to produce softly blended tones.

PAINTING 'ALLA PRIMA'

When we complete a painting in one session or 'one wet' it is said to be painted *alla prima* (from the Italian for 'at the first'). In normal circumstances it is possible to work on a painting for a day or so before its surface becomes unreceptive to new paint. *Alla-prima* painting is technically simple and because the time span is modest it is often easier to produce a result that is coherent and well structured. Because the paint goes on 'in one wet' it doesn't matter if it sinks a little as all the tones are adjusted together.

The spontaneity of working at speed, adapting as you go to accommodate changes of mind or variations in the lighting or view, is one of the great joys of oil painting. As it is technically relatively simple, it is best to try this method before going on to the more complex method of painting in layers.

To start painting *alla prima* you will need your oil colour squeezed out onto the palette, some turpentine in a dipper, a selection of brushes and a palette knife.

Painters vary very much in how they like to proceed next. Some will begin by working very thinly, gradually beefing up the density of the pigment as the image starts to become established. Others prefer to work rather more solidly straight away, using the paint undiluted with any solvent or medium. These choices will partly depend on whether you want to start by making drawn linear marks first or by blocking in the tonal masses and drawing back into this later with the brush. For myself, I would say that I vary my approach according to the subject and the conditions at the time.

Whichever way you work, make it a priority to cover the whole surface of the painting quickly rather than working in piecemeal fashion. This will enable you to think straight away about the composition as a whole and to check that on the scale on which you've chosen to work you'll get everything in.

I find it helpful to make small drawings in a sketchbook before starting to paint, to establish where the edges of the composition are going to be. If you are working on oil sketching paper the painting can be trimmed to the exact

Sky and Chesil Beach, oil on paper, 20 x 26 cm (8 x 10½ in). Oil sketching papers are available in a variety of surfaces and are ideal for painting 'in one wet'.

Evening Sky, Dillington,
20 x 22.5 cm (8 x 9 in).
One of three little boards
painted in one evening as
the sun sank through a
multi-layered sky. To cope
with such a fast-changing
situation you have to
remember what's just
happened, anticipate
changes and make
alterations as these occur.
Oil paint is the perfect
medium for making these
constant modifications
and revisions.

proportions that the drawing demands. If you
are working on a board or canvas you will need
to take into consideration its shape and
proportions before you start drawing.

Once you have the whole surface covered you
can push the paint around to a considerable
extent. You can work from the breadth of your
first strokes with a large brush down through
smaller sizes as you refine the image further. If
you reach a point where the painting starts to
look fussy or disjointed, wipe or scrape off the
colour and start again with bigger brushes.

You may find it quite difficult at first to build
up several layers of paint cleanly while working
wet-into-wet. By using the knife to gently scrape
away the surface of the paint, some of the image
will remain in the grain of the canvas but you
will have a fresh surface on which to work. So
long as you avoid building up a thick, unstable
layer you'll be able to carry on all day, gradually
building up a rich and complex web of colours
and tones.

EXERCISE

Placing touches of colour over an underlying layer of
wet oil paint, without muddying everything, takes
practice. Apply a wash of colour onto a board, then try
using a variety of brushes to apply a range of marks
on to the wet paint. You will find that holding the
brush well back from the ferrule, and at a low angle
(as though spreading butter on bread), allows you to
work very delicately.

Irises and Michaelmas Daisies (detail).
This detail from a finished painting shows how a variety of textures and paint thicknesses has been built up across the surface of the canvas.

▼ *Irises and Sunlight, Marrowbone*,
61 x 45.5 cm (24 x 18 in).
This image has been built in layers using quite thick paint (impasto) for the lighter areas and thin, transparent glazes for the darks.

WORKING IN LAYERS

Oil paint dries slowly, from the outside in, not by evaporation but by absorbing oxygen from the air. This simple fact determines much of what we can do with oil colours. Wet paint can be painted into and dry paint can be painted over, but semi-dry paint should not be painted over. What happens is that the surface of the paint skins over quite quickly but once this has happened the drying process slows down and the paint goes through a stage of becoming very absorbent. If you then apply further paint layers on top, the absorbent underlayer sucks oil from the fresh layers, leaving them starved and dull-looking. Thus if you need to continue with a painting beyond one session it is advisable to leave it until it is completely dry to the touch, and not at all tacky, before continuing. A very thick impasto layer may take months, even years, to dry right through, so you should avoid a thick build-up of paint in any area that you intend to overpaint.

'FAT OVER LEAN'

The most important basic rule in oil painting is to work 'fat over lean', particularly when building up a painting in layers. Put simply, this means that in the early stages you should use thin, fast-drying, 'lean' paint, diluted with turpentine and no oil; as you build up further layers of paint, gradually increase the proportion of oil to turpentine in your mixing medium, making the paint progressively 'fatter' and slower-drying.

The reason for this is that fat paint is more flexible than lean paint, and takes longer to dry. If lean paint is applied over fat, the top layer will dry before the lower, more oily one. As the lower layer dries it shrinks, and this movement causes the hardened upper layer to crack.

OILING OUT

When working on a painting over a period of time you may notice patches here and there where the colour appears matt and loses its brilliance. This is known as 'sinking', and is caused by the oil in the upper layers of paint being sucked out by the layers underneath. This problem can be solved by 'oiling out', which simply means replenishing the oil content of the paint by wiping it with a rag soaked in a mixture of 80 per cent linseed or stand oil with 20 per cent turpentine or white spirit. Leave the picture to dry for about a week before you overpaint.

Alternatively, retouching varnish can be used to revitalise the surface of the paint, and this can be overpainted as soon as it is dry.

Narcissi,
10 x 22 cm (4 x 8½ in).
By floating a pearly coloured glaze over most of this image, leaving only the two larger flowers left of centre untouched, I think I was able to enhance the impression of them pushing up into the light. A soft brush is best for glazing.

PRACTICAL TIP

Some colours, notably Titanium White and Cobalt Blue, dry more slowly than others and you can speed things up in the early stages of a painting by not using much of these colours in your mixtures.

PROJECT
PLAYING WITH PAINT

❖

Medium
Oil paint

❖

Colours
Titanium White
French Ultramarine
Venetian Red
Raw Sienna

❖

Support
Oil sketching paper

❖

Size
Approximately 30 x 38 cm
(12 x 15 in)

❖

Equipment
Selection of round and
filbert hog bristle brushes in
various sizes
Soft mop brush
Turpentine
Oil-painting medium
Palette
Painting knife
Cotton rags

❖

Time
Two hours initially plus one
hour later

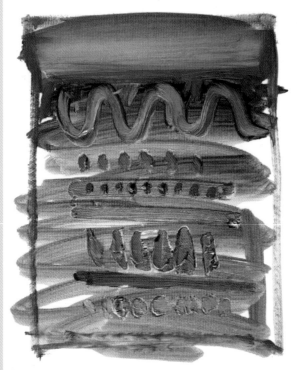

A thin wash of French Ultramarine, heavily diluted with turpentine, is the background for this little game with paint in which I've tried to place a variety of strokes of colour without disturbing the underlying wash.

For this first project I would like you to spend some time enjoying the visual and tactile qualities of oil paint without the constraint of worrying about making a finished image.

Using just the few colours I have suggested, or a limited palette of your own choice, begin by arranging the colours onto your palette. Squeeze out a reasonable quantity of paint, not just a spot of each colour. Pick up a little colour on a brush and try out different ways of putting it down on the paper. Light touches and firm ones will have contrasting characters. A smeared stroke is distinct from a single touch.

Try mixing colours together using the painting knife and adding a little turpentine to make the colour run and spread. Use the knife to build up a thick impasto. Experiment with building up a layer of colour, scraping or wiping it down and then placing light touches of paint over the top. Holding the brush very lightly, some way up the handle, will give you more control than gripping it tightly at the ferrule. Enjoy yourself as you discover what the paint is capable of.

When the paint is thoroughly dry, try building up further layers of colour to create a richer, more complex surface. Thin the paint down with oil-painting medium and practise laying thin, transparent glazes and semi-opaque scumbles. Notice how the underlying colours are modified by these thin films of colour, and how the rough and smooth surface textures of the underlying layers are emphasized.

Various colours have been put down, wiped or scraped off, scratched through and built layer upon layer while still wet. Thick and opaque or thin and transparent, oil paint can display so many fascinating qualities.

▼ Here a glaze of French Ultramarine has been brushed over dry colour displaying a variety of surface textures. The glaze medium here is about 30 per cent oil-painting medium, 70 per cent turpentine.

SELF-ASSESSMENT

✧ Have you produced a rich and varied paint surface?

✧ Did you work boldly, moving your arm from the shoulder and not the wrist?

✧ Did you manage to work cleanly, using the painting knife to do your mixing?

✧ Have you enjoyed yourself?

CHAPTER FOUR

DRAWING & COMPOSITION

I think all painters should draw in one form or another. For myself, an important part of the creative process happens in my sketchbook, in which I will make many hundreds of drawings in the course of a year. Drawing is an invaluable way of visualizing the thought processes that go into making a painting. Often, when considering a new subject I approach it initially through a series of sketches and drawings. The first of these may be primarily concerned with thinking my way through the 'mechanics' of the subject, trying to understand the shapes of the individual elements and how they relate to one another. Then I make thumbnail sketches in which I try out alternative compositions and try to think ahead to imagine the effect that tone and colour are going to have. Throughout this preliminary stage I'm conscious that I'm absorbing the subject and storing up ideas that will surface later on in the painting itself.

Different drawing media will stress different elements of the subject being drawn. For example, using a steel nib and black ink will emphasize the linear aspects of a subject, whereas charcoal will stress the tonal masses. Thus the choice of a particular drawing medium may be an unconscious form of selection as the characteristics of the drawing may well be carried over into the painting.

Drawn with a mapping pen and ink, the stress in this study is on the linear and structural aspects of the subject.

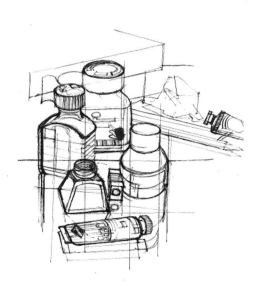

In contrast, soft graphite stick emphasizes tonal masses and three-dimensional form.

Drawing for
Quimper Flower Market.
One of several
sketchbook
drawings I made
of this fascinating
subject.

▼ *Quimper Flower Market*, 40 x 56 cm (16 x 22 in). The tables with their buckets of flowers and the little squares of light shining through the skylights were the starting point for this composition, which began as a group of drawings in a sketchbook.

COMPARATIVE MEASURING

One of the functions of drawing as a preliminary to painting is to establish the composition and ensure that the proportions are accurate. Taking frequent comparative measurements is a good way to check on the proportions as you draw. Use your pencil as a measuring tool to compare the length of one part of your subject to the length of another part so you have an idea of their relative sizes.

Comparative measuring is a useful aid to drawing by eye because it helps you to draw what you see, not what you know. To demonstrate this, find a subject that has some depth to it, such as a street scene or a landscape view. Draw part of the foreground in outline, then move your eye to some small part of the background and draw that. When you check by measuring you will probably find that you have made the foreground section too small and the background section too large. If this has happened, don't worry, it's just an example of your eye being deceived by the effect of perspective on scale.

I enjoyed making this drawing in soft charcoal pencil as a preliminary to painting the subject. Notice the way the foreground is made up of large, open shapes and the horizon is crammed with detail.

EXERCISE

An easy way to practise using the measuring technique is to choose a subject which is broadly two-dimensional and includes plenty of horizontal and vertical angles and lines. Examples might include the façade of a building, or a wall lined with bookshelves and pictures.

Keep your arm locked, one eye closed and hold your thumbnail against the pencil to mark the measurements exactly.

HOW TO MEASURE

To practise comparative measuring choose a subject with plenty of horizontals and verticals, such as a group of buildings or an interior. Look for a convenient dimension to use as your yardstick – say, the height of a door.

Hold your pencil near the base so that most of it extends vertically. Hold it at arm's length, elbow locked, and line it up with the door so that the pencil tip coincides with the top. Keeping your head still and one eye closed, slide your thumbnail down the pencil until it coincides with the bottom of the door. Keeping your thumbnail in place and your arm locked, move the pencil to another part of the subject and compare its length with the length of your key measurement (you can measure horizontally in the same way by turning your pencil through 90 degrees). To measure consistently, stand with your feet in the same position and your arm fully extended each time; if you bend your arm your measurements will be inaccurate.

Work across your drawing, frequently checking key measurements and transferring them to your paper. Gradually a web of lines will develop out of which the drawing will grow. It does not matter if your drawing is proportionately larger or smaller than the subject at the end of your pencil. What this method achieves is to ensure that the relationships between the various elements of the subject are accurate.

In this drawing I used the proportions of the foreground door as the key measurement. All other dimensions were compared with the width of the open doorway. If you haven't used the comparative measuring technique before, start off with a simple subject such as the façade of a building before progressing to a subject viewed in perspective.

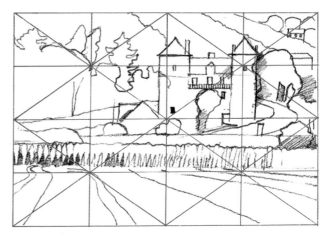

▲ Make sure your drawing is rectangular, then draw in the two diagonals with a ruler. The point where the lines cross is the centre, and a horizontal and vertical line drawn through this point divides the drawing into four equal rectangles.

▲ Add the second diagonal to each of the four rectangles. Then draw the horizontal and vertical lines, dividing the drawing into 16 equal rectangles.

▼ Repeat the process once more to arrive at the 8 x 8 grid shown here.

ENLARGING FROM A DRAWING

Sometimes when you draw a subject with real energy and engagement you will intuitively hit on a composition that really works. This may be because the shapes and masses relate together in a pleasing way, but may also have something to do with the way one area is emphasized by the particular way in which it has been drawn. However, I have often watched students develop an exciting compositional idea through a preliminary drawing, only to see that idea watered down in the finished painting. It may simply be that they've got it out of their system through the drawing and lack the stamina to do it all again; but most often it is because something goes wrong with the proportions when translating the drawing onto the canvas. For example, I've seen students make a 'portrait' format drawing and then try to draw it up on a 'landscape' format canvas, or make a drawing in the proportions of, say, 3:4 and then transfer it to a canvas whose proportions are 5:6.

The most reliable way of transferring a drawing, particularly when you need to enlarge or reduce it to fit the canvas, is by squaring-up. There are various methods, but I find the following is the easiest.

Draw a line round your drawing, making sure its corners are square (if you prefer not to mark the drawing, lay a sheet of tracing paper or clear acetate over it and work on that). Locate the centre of the drawing by ruling two diagonal lines from corner to corner, then draw a vertical and a horizontal line through the point where they cross.

Now repeat the process in each of the four corners of the square. Keep doing this until you have eight rows of eight rectangles covering your drawing.

Line up your drawing with the bottom left corner of your painting support and use a pencil

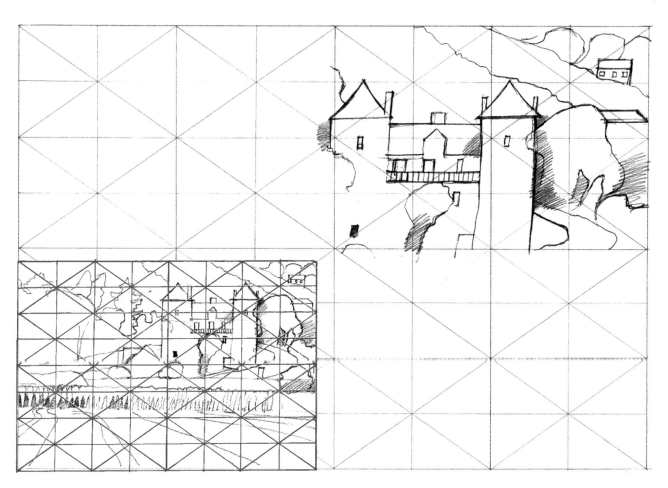

and a long straight-edge to extend the longest diagonal line on the drawing right across until it cuts the top edge of the support. Drop a vertical line from this point; everything beyond it will be waste and can be cut off.

Remove the original drawing and repeat the sequence of diagonal, vertical and horizontal lines on the painting support until once again you have eight rows of eight rectangles.

Now simply copy what is in each rectangle of the drawing onto the corresponding rectangle on the painting support.

▲ Lay the drawing exactly over one corner of the new surface and extend the long diagonal as shown. Any rectangle drawn on this diagonal will have the same proportion as the original drawing. Repeat the grid on the new surface and copy the drawing one small rectangle at a time.

PRACTICAL TIP

Sometimes familiarity with your painting makes it hard to see any flaws in its composition. Look at the painting in a mirror, or turn it upside down, and all will be revealed!

Good composition is largely an instinctive thing and really about balancing or contrasting one area against another so that the picture knits together, is pleasing to the eye and combines harmony with variety.

Introduce stability through harmonies of shape, colour and tone, but at the same time think about various kinds of compositional contrast that will enliven the picture. For example, horizontal and vertical elements in a painting give symmetry and stability and can be set off by active, organic shapes. Introduce small accents of bright colour in a largely neutral painting, or strong contrasts of tone that draw attention to a particular area. Play off passive shapes against active shapes and give the viewer's eye places to rest within a composition as well as areas of excitement. Most importantly, try to have one main focus of interest in a painting, with everything else secondary to it, and organize these elements so as to lead the eye into, and not out of, the picture.

Above all, learn from the examples of good painting in this book and from your own experiments; don't rely on any 'magic' formula as a substitute for your own judgement.

Sketchbook drawing. The selection of this particular viewpoint allowed me to exploit the amusing contrast between the grand, heroic horseman and the modern, but mandane, motorbikes. By making sketchbook drawings one can quickly evaluate the possibilities of a subject.

COMPOSING THE PICTURE

Art-instruction books often present numerous 'rules' about how to compose a picture, but on the whole I find these rather unhelpful and they can be misleading, especially when illustrated with line drawings. Painting isn't necessarily as edgy as that and blocks of tone and colour and the way the main shapes and masses interlock are more important to the overall structure than are lines.

However, to say that the rules are unhelpful is not to say that composition itself doesn't matter. A well-composed painting will arrest your attention even before you have understood what the subject is and will continue to hold your attention as you begin to unravel its intricacies.

USING A VIEWFINDER

As much as anything, composing a picture is about choosing the best viewpoint, and this is where a viewfinder comes in useful. A viewfinder is simply a piece of card, ideally black, with a rectangular hole cut in it. The edges of the viewfinder act as a 'window frame' which isolates one section of the subject so you can see it more clearly in terms of composition. Close one eye and look through the viewfinder, moving it this way and that, toward and away from you until the subject is framed in a pleasing way.

To make a viewfinder you will need a sheet of black card, a ruler, a craft knife and a pencil. Draw a rectangle in the centre of the sheet to the same proportions as the support on which you intend to paint. Cut out the window, and your viewfinder is ready for use.

PRACTICAL TIP

Make your viewfinder a little larger in size than is sometimes recommended, enabling it to be held at arm's length; that way you will find it less of a strain to focus simultaneously on the inner edge of the viewfinder and the view it contains. It is useful to have several viewfinders in a variety of proportions.

Jason Bowyer,
Lemon Tree,
91 x 107 cm (36 x 42 in).
Jason Bowyer's fine draughtsmanship and compositional skill are clearly demonstrated in the way that this image unfolds from the lefthand side across to the right, inviting the viewer to 'read' it like the page of a book.

CHAPTER FIVE

ABOUT TONE

An understanding of tones – the lights and darks – is essential to the success of a painting, particularly if you are interested in capturing the effects of light on your subjects. Tone and colour are, of course, intimately linked, but I want to concentrate purely on tone in this chapter because it is an area that causes confusion among painters of all abilities.

The distribution of lights, darks and mid tones is the glue that holds an image together. It is through the use of tonal contrasts that we are able to describe three-dimensional form, create the illusion of depth and space, establish rhythm and harmony in the composition, and convey mood and atmosphere. When planning and painting a picture, the tones should be given careful consideration. If a painting contains too many different tones it becomes rather confused and disjointed and the emotional message becomes dissipated.

▶ *Fantails, Morning Light,* 76 x 63.5 cm (30 x 25 in)

Tom Coates, *Venice at Night,* 51 x 61 cm (20 x 24 in). An object lesson in how less often says more, this is a very tonal painting in a limited range of colours. By getting the tones absolutely right, Tom Coates gives us an immediate sensation of being in the Piazzetta on a wet evening.

Road to the Cobb,
Lyme Regis,
15 x 28cm (6 x 11in).
I had stumbled upon this subject just as the light was moving out to the right, and returned the next day in time to capture it on canvas. What excited me was the cool bluish tone of the white buildings, backlit by the glare of the sun's reflection on the sea; the challenge lay in assessing the temperature and intensity of the colours as well as getting the tones just right.

LOOKING FOR TONES

The word 'tone' refers to the lightness or darkness of an area, regardless of its colour. Every colour has a tonal value, somewhere on a scale between almost white and almost black. In a black and white photograph a yellow object may appear almost white while a blue object appears grey. Judging the tonal value of coloured objects requires some practice as the hues and intensities of some colours – particularly bright ones – are difficult to define tonally. You may recognize an orange as being intense and warm in colour, but is it light or dark in tone? The very intensity of the colour can trick your eye into seeing the tone of the orange as lighter or darker than it really is.

To add to the confusion, colours and tones are modified by the prevailing light. For example, backlighting will lower the tone of an object considerably even if it is light in colour, and the effect of aerial perspective means that a darker coloured object in the distance may actually appear lighter in tone than a comparatively pale object in the foreground.

Looking at your subject through half-closed eyes can help you to judge tones more accurately, as this cuts down the detail and reduces the subject to simple shapes whose relative tonal values become more obvious.

With practice you will find it becomes easier to make these tonal judgments. A good mental exercise is to look at a view and try to number the different tones on a scale of one to 10, ranging from the lightest to the darkest.

TONAL RELATIONSHIPS

Your eye's ability to adjust to different levels of light by dilating and contracting the pupil can be a problem if you concentrate for too long on one area in isolation; your eye may be deceived into thinking that the area is higher or lower in tone than is actually the case. To assess the tones accurately you need to keep looking at one tone in relation to another. Relax your eye by moving your gaze quickly from one point to another and back again; this will help you make comparisons before your pupil has time to dilate or contract.

Just about everything in painting is a matter of establishing relationships. When making colour and tonal judgments it is important to think of the painting as a whole and not as a series of isolated sections. Always work from the general to the particular, establishing the bigger relationships first and working down to the smaller ones. In a landscape, for instance, there may be a whole section such as the sky

Willow Wands and Ironstone Plate, 92 x 61 cm (36 x 24 in). Backlighting simplifies and strengthens the tonal pattern of this subject. Notice the counterchange of dark shapes against the light from the window and light shapes against the dark tone of the wall.

that has a variety of tones within it, but which is still tonally lighter overall than the landscape below. It is important to establish these major relationships right at the start, and not allow yourself to get side-tracked into worrying about detail that can be dealt with in the later stages.

This process links well with the idea of starting broadly, with big brushes, and finishing with smaller ones. Oil paint, more than any other medium, allows you to state the whole image simply and quickly and then lets you refine it further, lightening or darkening a passage until you get the relationships right.

▶ Mary Jackson,
*Emily in the Shade of
the Trees*,
36 x 46 cm (14 x 18 in).
Although the little girl is quite
small and half-hidden by
foliage, she commands
attention because she is
placed in the centre of the
composition and the light
tones of her clothing contrast
with the deeper tones around
her. The painting is
beautifully structured tonally
and the subtle diagonals and
tilting lines act as a foil to the
frieze-like nature of the
composition.

▲ *Walkers and Sitters*,
20 x 25 cm (8 x 9¾ in).
Painted at the end of a warm
afternoon, the starting point
for this study was the
wonderful hazy light and the
close tones typical of this time
of the day.

TONAL KEY

The term tonal key refers to the overall lightness
or darkness of a painting. It is useful to think in
terms of tonal key when planning a painting,
because this will help to determine its mood. A
high-key painting contains mainly light tones
and colours, and few strong contrasts of tone.
Such a painting may convey a feeling of
lightness and brightness, or softness and delicacy.
The Impressionists most often used high-key
colours in their sun-drenched landscapes.

A low-key painting contains mainly tones from
the darker end of the scale. Such an image can
convey many moods, from dramatic and
disturbing to calm and restful.

Turner worked with the
natural tonality of colours in
many of his mature oil
paintings and watercolours.
By using yellow in the lightest
areas and blue in the darker
ones, he was able to keep the
colour vibrant throughout the
entire tonal range. Here I
have made a freely painted
variation on one of these
subjects (*Norham Castle*,
painted around 1845) to try
to see how it works.

TONE AND COMPOSITION

The way in which areas of tone are disposed across the picture surface is an important underlying current in the composition of a picture. If you squint at a painting through half-closed eyes you will see it reduced to its very simple components – almost an abstract. Invariably a good painting will be divided into just a few areas of light and dark, creating a strong and unified image.

Strong tonal contrasts tend to attract the eye and so can be used to create emphasis where you want it in the picture. Reserve the strongest contrasts for the main focal point while keeping the contrasts elsewhere relatively subdued.

Patterns of light and dark tone created by sunlight and shadow can give life and energy to the picture by setting up subtle rhythms and connections that lead the eye through the composition in a pleasing way. Bear this in mind when painting landscapes; you will find that early morning and late afternoon produce the most interesting shadows, whereas at midday there is very little shadow around.

Another way of using tone to animate a picture is through 'counterchange' the placing of light shapes against dark, and dark shapes against light. These light/dark reversals set up interesting contrasts for the viewer to explore, and act as visual 'stepping stones' that create rhythm and movement.

PROJECT
TONE INTO COLOUR

✧

Medium
Oil paint

✧

Colours
Titanium White, Lemon Yellow, Cadmium Yellow, Raw Sienna, Cadmium Scarlet, Permanent Rose, French Ultramarine, Coeruleum Blue, Terre Verte, Chrome Oxide Green, Raw Umber

✧

Support
Oil sketching paper prepared with a thin wash of Terre Verte and allowed to dry

✧

Size
51 x 38 cm (20 x 15 in)

✧

Equipment
Selection of round, flat and filbert hog bristle brushes in various sizes
One or two small round sable or synthetic soft hair brushes
Palette
Dipper
Palette knife
Easel
Thin stick of charcoal
Fixative spray
Turpentine

✧

Time
About two hours for the first painting and four hours for the second

This two-part project is designed to help you to see colours in terms of their tonal value. This is an important aspect of painting, because it is by balancing the tonal 'weight' of one colour against another that we achieve both harmony and variety in our paintings. In the project you will make two paintings from one still-life group – the first in monochrome and the second in full colour.

Assemble a collection of brightly coloured objects and arrange them on a table. Try to include a variety of geometric and rounded forms. Illuminate the group with a desk lamp to create a steady light that casts descriptive patterns of light and shadow. Position yourself so that you can see the whole group at once. Spend a few minutes observing the group and assessing the light, medium and dark tones.

Squeeze out some Titanium White and Raw Umber onto your palette and use the palette knife to mix a sequence of tones ranging from pure white (the lightest) down to pure umber (the darkest). Mix an odd number of tones – say five or seven – so that there's one in the middle. Sketch out your composition using charcoal and give it a light spray with fixative, or knock back the excess charcoal by flicking with a rag. Place a brush stroke of pure white at the point you judge to be lightest in tone and pure Raw

▼ A seven-step tonal scale from pure white to pure raw umber. Laying out pre-mixed tones like these on your palette would be a good starting point for the tonal study.

Umber at the darkest. Now start placing patches of tone across the paper to indicate the main tonal steps. Gradually fill in with the subtle intermediate tones, constantly assessing and revising your judgments until the paper is covered and you are happy with the result.

For your second painting, use the full range of colours listed left. As you mix each colour you see in front of you, use your first painting as a reference when judging its tonal value. As in the first version be very sparing in your use of pure white; it is likely that only one or two areas may be bright enough to warrant its use. As before, mix small dabs of colour and put these down as reference points. The painting will develop quite slowly, but resist the temptation to finish one part before moving on to the next. Instead, keep your eye moving across the subject and make constant comparisons between one part of the subject and another.

◄ It can be very instructive to paint without reference to colour. Here I've set up a little group of brightly coloured odds and ends from around the studio and painted it using only mixtures of raw umber and white. Notice how the boundaries between objects disappear when they are similar in tone.

The painting above shows a similar group of objects, this time painted in full colour. I tried to keep the colour vibrant and saturated without losing sight of the tonal structure of my little group.

SELF-ASSESSMENT

✧ Did you half-close your eyes to assess the tones more accurately?

✧ Did you manage to achieve an even gradation of tones from light to dark when mixing the colours for the tonal study?

✧ Look at your two paintings together. Has the tonal study helped you make sense of the relative tonal values of the colours?

CHAPTER SIX

COLOUR

The strong density of pigment in good-quality oil paints, coupled with their unique optical qualities, gives a special depth and richness to the colours brushed onto the canvas. At the same time, the most delicate pale tints can be achieved by mixing the colours with white. And because what you see on the palette is what you get in the painting, you don't have to make allowances for the colours lightening as they dry, as you do with water-based media.

But just how do you translate the myriad colours in the visual world into mixtures of just a few pigments on a palette? Well, you probably can't, but you can get close. Formulas for mixtures are of no value; what is important is your individual response to colours and your understanding of how they behave and how they interact with each other.

▶ *Daffodils and Blue Pansies*, 45 x 41 cm (18 x 16 in)

Bo Hilton, *The Light Shop*, 51 x 61 cm (20 x 24 in)

COURTESY OF MANYA IGEL FINE ARTS LTD

There is a great sense of the artist's enjoyment of his subject here, and a delicate balance between the quietly painted foreground figures and the brilliant colour behind them.

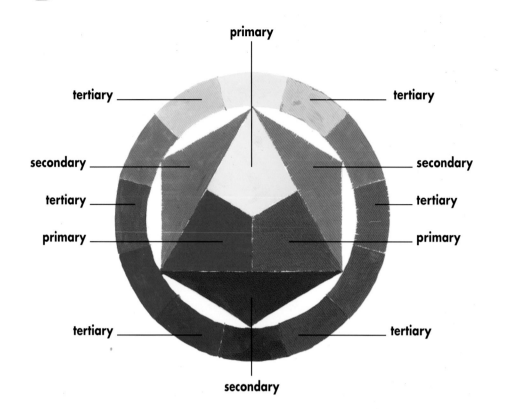

primary

tertiary — — — tertiary

secondary — secondary

tertiary — — tertiary

primary — — primary

tertiary — — tertiary

secondary

This colour wheel shows the basic pigment colours and their combinations. In the centre triangle are the primary colours. Around the triangle are the secondary colours, made by mixing two primaries (e.g. yellow and blue make green). The outer rim of the wheel shows how the tertiary colours are mixed from a primary and a secondary (e.g. red and violet make red-violet).

THE COLOUR WHEEL

The colour wheel is a simplified version of the spectrum, showing the arrangement of primary and secondary colours from which all other colours are mixed. In practice the colour wheel is not the best guide when it comes to mixing actual paints because artists' pigments, unlike the colours of light, are not pure. However, it is a convenient device which helps us to understand and visualize how colours relate to each other and what, in theory, happens when they are mixed.

The version above shows just 12 secondary and tertiary colours, but you can see that by making the subdivisions finer, an infinite number of colours can be obtained, and if you mix any of these colours with white to make tints you begin to appreciate the possibilities of the system.

PRIMARY COLOURS
Pure red, yellow and blue cannot be mixed from other colours and so are called primary colours.

SECONDARY COLOURS
These are obtained by mixing two primary

colours. Thus green, orange and violet are secondaries.

TERTIARY COLOURS
These are obtained by mixing a primary and a secondary colour together. The tertiaries are red-violet, blue-violet, blue-green, yellow-green, yellow-orange and red-orange.

COMPLEMENTARY COLOURS
Colours which lie opposite each other on the colour wheel are called complementary colours. When juxtaposed they intensify each other.

NEUTRAL COLOURS
When two complementaries are mixed together they neutralize each other to create a range of neutral browns and greys. Mixing three primaries also produces neutral colours. Knowing how to mix this group is at the heart of good painting.

HARMONIOUS COLOURS
These are next to each other on the colour wheel. They share a common base colour – for example, blue-green, blue and blue-violet all have blue in common.

TALKING ABOUT COLOUR

So many of the words that have a precise meaning when applied to colour also have a more general usage that it's worth just defining what is meant by certain colour terms.

HUE
This is the name of a colour in its purest form – red, green, blue or yellow, for example.

TONE
This refers to the lightness or darkness of a colour, independent of its hue.

LOCAL COLOUR
This describes the actual colour of something, independent of the effect of the ambient light. The local colour of an apple may be green, but in bright sunlight the lit side may appear yellowish and the shadow side reddish.

TINT
A tint is a mixture of any colour with white.

SHADE
A shade is a mixture of any colour with black. In practice, adding black is not the best way to darken a colour as it has a deadening effect.

INTENSITY
Sometimes called 'saturation', this refers to the purity or brilliance of a colour. Colours can be de-saturated by mixing them with white or with their complementary (opposite) colour.

TEMPERATURE
Put simplistically, reds, oranges and yellows are said to be 'warm' while blues, violets and greens are 'cool'.

▲ A wide range of subtle secondary hues can be obtained simply by mixing pairs of primaries in different proportions.

When complementary colours are mixed they neutralize each other. The centre square on each of these charts is a 50-50 mix of two complementaries, resulting in a neutral grey or brown.

The brushmarks here are exactly the same colour, but the colour looks more vibrant and higher in key against the coloured ground than against the white ground.

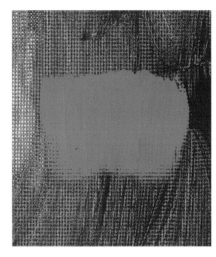

HOW COLOURS INTERACT

Using colour is not as simple as knowing how to mix primaries and secondaries. During the course of making a painting you will realize that colours can never be regarded in isolation because they are influenced by the colours around them. As one colour is put down it will alter the appearance of another colour, and so painting is a continuous process of balancing, judging, altering and refining. A bright colour appears even brighter when placed next to a muted one, a warm colour appears warmer when placed next to a cool one, and a light tone appears even lighter when placed next to a dark one. You will even find that a flat area of colour looks different to a textured one.

Similarly, the warmth or coolness of a colour does not exist in isolation. It is generally held that reds, oranges and yellows are 'warm' colours while blues, greens and violets are 'cool'. However, there are varying degrees of warmth and coolness within both of these groups. Permanent Rose, for example, is a cooler red than Cadmium Red; French Ultramarine is a warmer blue than Coeruleum Blue; and Sap Green is warmer than Viridian. Whilst it is acknowledged that warm colours appear to advance and cool colours recede, in practice they do so only in relative terms. Thus the distant hills in a landscape painting will only appear to recede if the colours in the foreground are sufficiently warm to provide the necessary contrast.

Many artists set out the colours on their palette in a systematic order running from warm to cool.

LOCAL AND OBSERVED COLOUR

As with so many things in painting, our perception of colour can be hampered by relying on what we know rather than what we see. I know that a field is green, but when I see it late in the evening as a dark slab beneath a luminous sky it may not appear green at all. It is all too easy in these circumstances to paint the field the colour I know it to be, and the result would fail to convey what I am trying to say about evening light.

Another problem that confronts the novice painter is how to model form of an object by darkening the local colour as it turns into shadow and lightening it as it turns to the light. If you're painting a green apple resting in a white cloth, for example, it's no good adding black to darken the colour on the shadow side – the colour produced will be like mud. But if you adjust the colour towards its complementary, red, you will be on the right lines.

You'll notice, too, that the darkest part of the apple is just inside the edge and that reflected light from the white cloth lightens the dark side. If the white cloth is removed and a coloured one put in its place you will see that the reflected light in the shadow takes on this colour. Within a still-life group, or indeed any subject, colours will be bounced around and reflected off each other and a sensitivity to this will help to give your paintings a sense of unity.

▲ Lit from one side, this green apple displays its local colour only in one or two small areas. As the form turns away from the light the colour takes on some of its complementary, red. The shadow side is lit by reflected light from the white table.

The same apple, this time on a pink cloth. Notice how the pink of the cloth is reflected on the underside of the apple and the green of the apple is picked up within the cast shadow.

EXERCISE

Place two or three simple objects close together on a sheet of white paper and light the group from one side. Make a painting, being as faithful as you can to what you see. Look for reflected colour both in the objects and on the white paper. You'll find that the shadows, in particular, are full of colour.

A LIMITED PALETTE

The palette of three colours suggested below (plus Titanium White for mixing tints) is very much a low-key palette. Truly brilliant colour effects cannot be achieved using just these colours. However, it is much easier to achieve a feeling of harmony and unity with such a restricted range and its a great way to start learning how to get the most from your colours.

FROM THE TOP:
**Raw Sienna,
Venetian Red,
French Ultramarine**

A WIDER PALETTE

Colour theory tells us that if we have the three primary colours plus white in optically pure pigment, any colour can be mixed from them. In practice, although much can be done with a limited palette, available pigments in oil don't quite mimic the pure optical primaries. They each tend to have a bias towards another colour and this is why colour theory sometimes lets us down.

My usual working palette now has about twelve colours. By including a warm and a cool version of each of the primaries and adding some secondary colours, a wider range of mixtures can be achieved. By widening the range slightly to include a 'hot' red and a 'cool' one, you have the added bonus that one is transparent while the other is opaque. This is where you can learn much by experience. You may like to try out my palette, listed here, only adding extra colours if they will enable you to do something more. Even with so few colours it is possible to mix an astonishing range of hues and tones, and in addition you can mix a range of subtle tints by mixing with white (Titanium White is cool and opaque, and the easiest to

begin with). The transparent nature of Raw Sienna and French Ultramarine make it easy to achieve very dark tones.

FROM THE TOP:
Lemon Yellow: cool, transparent yellow
Cadmium Yellow Deep: hot, dense yellow
Raw Sienna: earthy dark transparent yellow/brown
Venetian Red: opaque rusty red
Cadmium Scarlet: brilliant orange/red
Permanent Rose: cool transparent bluish red
French Ultramarine: strong violet blue, transparent
Cerulean Blue: greenish blue
Oxide of Chromium: very opaque earthy green
Terre Verte: transparent earth green
Raw Umber: dark grey/brown

COLOUR KEY

You can decide when you start a painting how high you are going to pitch the key. This is partly a matter of tone but as I said in the last chapter, the two topics are intimately connected. Remember, the range of colours and tones at your disposal is large, but nothing like what you see in nature. Pitching the key low will give you more room to spell out the subtlety of colour at the light end of the scale, but at the expense of compressing the tones at the lower end. If pitched too high, a still life with brilliantly lit yellow flowers may appear washed out because there are not enough darker colours to provide contrast. On the whole it's a good idea to key the tonal scale around a bright colour that you want to give its true tonal and colour value and work out from there. Now this

Crowds on Weymouth Promenade, 30.5 x 35.5 cm (12 x 14 in). Sunlight transmitted through the deckchairs and splashing across the ground makes this a contrasty and high-key subject.

isn't as difficult as it seems, but it does mean you have to decide at the outset which part of the subject interests you most.

OPTICAL MIXING

The Impressionist painters discovered that with their high-key palette the brilliance of their colour effects could be enhanced by painting with loosely applied strokes of pure colour. When seen from a distance, these strokes appeared to merge into one mass of colour, but the effect was more vibrant than that created by a solid area of blended colour. The reason for this is that the small, separate flecks of colour 'vibrate' on the retina of the eye and appear to shimmer. These ideas were taken further by Georges Seurat, whose pointillist, or divisionist,

method broke all colour into its components. Separate dots of primary colours like blue and yellow, for instance, were intended to 'fuse' in the eye as green.

On the right hand side of this little study, some of the colour mixing is left to be completed in the eye of the observer.

PROJECT
HIGH KEY/LOW KEY

✧

Medium
Oil paint

✧

Colours
Titanium White, Lemon Yellow, Cadmium Yellow, Raw Sienna, Cadmium Scarlet, Permanent Rose, French Ultramarine, Coeruleum Blue, Terre Verte, Chrome Oxide Green, Raw Umber

✧

Surface
Painting boards prepared with a mid-toned imprimatura

✧

Size
Approximately 20 x 25 cm (8 x 10 in)

✧

Equipment
Your outdoor painting kit

✧

Time
An hour for each painting

North from Eggardon, Autumn,
46 x 51 cm
(18 x 20 in).
Fast-moving cumulus clouds and their shadows, and the wind in the trees, made this a subject full of movement. The road and hedge snaking down into the valley lead the eye into the distance and help create a sense of three-dimensional space. The colour is quite saturated and the mass of the land is rather close in tone to that of the sky.

For this project I would like you to work on location and make two paintings from the same landscape subject, ideally on the same day. Make the first painting during the afternoon in strong sunlight. You will probably find that although the sky is the brightest area of the composition, there is much colour in the landscape itself that is at once light in tone and quite saturated in colour. By working on a board already covered with a veil of colour, you should avoid the trap of pitching your tones too high so that the picture appears pale and chalky.

The second painting should be made around dusk. If you're lucky the sky will be quite luminous in colour at this time of the day, with a much bigger tonal step down to the darkening landscape below. Notice how there is now much less contrast between the tones of the landscape than there was in the afternoon, and how much of the detail is suppressed. One of the frustrations of painting in the evening is that the subject reaches its greatest beauty and subtlety at around the time it becomes almost impossible to see the painting!

▲ *Crossed Vapour Trails,*
15 x 35.5 cm
(6 x 14 in).
I was already working on this little painting when the

second of the jets left its signature across the first one. The view of the beach and the cliffs beyond is darkened but the sun below the horizon is making the sky very three dimensional and rich in colour.

*Evening Sky Clearing
After Rain,*
25.5 x 20 cm
(10 x 8 in).
A small panel, one of several made during the course of an evening as the sky darkened. I've chosen an

upright format and a low horizon so that the subtle gradations of colour in the sky can be fully explored. Notice how the land is darkened and detail suppressed as tones are brought close together.

SELF-ASSESSMENT

✧ Does each of your paintings capture the feeling of a particular time of day?

✧ Does your painting of the evening landscape stand up to scrutiny in the cold light of the following morning? It takes practice to get used to an unfamiliar palette in failing light!

✧ Did you manage to indicate a sense of depth in the dark mass of the evening landscape?

CHAPTER SEVEN

STILL LIFE & INTERIORS

Not surprisingly, painters often produce their most personal and intimate work around still-life and interior subjects, recording their daily domestic life in a sort of visual diary. These subjects are always intensely interesting because they force us to look afresh at objects which are so familiar that they are often taken for granted.

Still-life and interior subjects are ideal for newcomers to the medium because, unlike landscapes, they allow you to paint or draw every day, whatever the weather and in the peace and privacy of your own space. They also allow you, the artist, to be in complete control. You can choose the objects you like and arrange them in a way that you find personally satisfying. Working in these controlled conditions, you can study at leisure the intricacies of colour and tone, form and space without having to cope with distractions.

There is a wealth of inspiration to be found in still lifes and interiors; they can, after all, range from intimate little studies of humble objects, through mini 'landscapes' to the vast interior space of a cathedral.

▶ Ken Howard, *Inside Looking Out*, 102 x 61 cm (40 x 24 in). I love the way the space continues through the window, linking the interior of the studio to the street and the gardens beyond. There are so many lessons in this superb painting: the seemingly casual composition, the confidence and rightness of each drawn mark and the exquisite tonal judgements.

Lilies at Marrowbone, 63 x 76 cm (25 x 30 in). This was painted in afternoon light, making use of the rectangle of sunlight from the window above. I liked the way that the various elements fell into horizontal bands, from the window, the outspread lilies and so on down to the sunlit edge of the table.

▶ *Daffodils and Little Bottles,*
25.5 x 30.5 cm (10 x 12 in).
Somebody had put these
large daffodil flowers into
little bottles, one in each. I
liked the way the flower
heads appeared to be
suspended as one didn't
immediately see the glass
bottles in the shadowy light
There are some postcards at
the back that give the
composition a sort of
framework.

◀ *Sid's Rocker and
Yellow Pansies,*
56 x 41 cm (22 x 18 in).
This one's a real 'clutter'
painting. I noticed this view
through an internal window.
There were pansies in a jar
on the window sill and
beyond it a very untidy
studio, but something about
the relationship between the
three windows at the back,
the rocking horse and all the
bits of furniture made me
want to paint it.

'FOUND' GROUPS

Probably the most difficult aspect of painting
still life is deciding initially what to paint. Once
you begin to think beyond the clichéd image of
wine bottles, fruit and flowers of traditional
still-life painting, the range of subjects is almost
limitless. Look around your home and select
objects that you like and find visually exciting.
You will certainly paint with more conviction if
you choose things that are meaningful to you.

More often than not you will just happen to
come across a ready-made situation that strikes
you as having the makings of a painting. With
me this often seems to happen after long
familiarity with the subject in question. It might
be a view through a half-open door from one
room into another, or a few small objects
casually arranged on a table. For me these
'found' subjects have a particular charm of
their own, combining the elements familiarity
and surprise.

At other times you may have to stage manage things a little more, but it is best to avoid over-complicated arrangements as they can appear contrived. Try to set things up in a casual way so that they appear to be entirely spontaneous and natural.

ORDER OUT OF CHAOS

There are three tables in my studio. In the way that stationary, flat surfaces do, they tend to accumulate all sorts of painting debris. I have several boxes of objects that I have enjoyed painting before, and much of the contents of these boxes is out on the tables or surrounding floor at any one time. I also like to keep fruit and flowers around the studio for the accents of bright colour they can provide.

The familiarity of each table and the world which it supports allows me to make minor adjustments or additions to a grouping without making it appear too contrived. Having the

tables standing out in the room rather than against the wall allows each group to be seen 'in the round', and sometimes something that hasn't worked from one direction is suddenly enlivened by a change of viewpoint.

Most often, however, it is the unplanned incident that gets me painting. My little girl brings in a brightly coloured toy and unknowingly abandons it in just the right place, or I'll dump a pile of drawings on the table for want of anywhere else to put them. A circuit of each table with a drawing pad enables me to explore some of the possibilities offered by each view. I will only allow myself to make changes in the layout of each table when I have explored all its possibilities. Still life painting tackled in this way is very like working from landscape, where I can delight in the familiarity of my surroundings while being constantly alert to the changes of lighting, season or habitation that make me want to record what I see.

◄ Strong side light creates a long cast shadow on the opposite side of the object.

▶ With the light source directly above, the cup seems to sit in a puddle of its own shadow.

CONTROLLING THE LIGHT

Working indoors in your own space, you can choose to illuminate your still lifes and interiors with either natural daylight or artificial light, or even a combination of both. You can also control the amount and direction of the light simply by opening and closing curtains or by moving lamps around. When painting indoor subjects you will soon become aware of the different moods and effects created by altering the strength and direction of the light, and what you learn will stand you in good stead when you are painting landscapes and trying to cope with the changeable light outdoors.

Working at night or with the curtains tightly drawn, collect some objects that you like and scatter them across a small table. Place a lamp to one side of your group and quite low down (an anglepoise lamp is excellent for this as you can point it just where you like). Working with a broad medium such as charcoal, graphite stick, ink wash or thinned oil paint on a large brush, make a small tonal study of the group. Pay close attention to the direction and depth of the cast shadows and the way they fall across neighbouring objects.

Now move the lamp to a position directly above the objects and repeat the exercise. The individual objects will seem to be floating on

Can you tell where the light source is situated here?

their own pools of shadow. Try placing the lamp in a variety of different positions and make a series of studies, noting how the patterns of light and shadow change each time. For example, when the group is lit from directly in front the shadows are behind the objects and the objects themselves appear flat and almost two-dimensional. When light falls on the group from slightly above and to one side (known as three-quarter lighting) it creates a strong impression of form and volume as well as picking out details of surface texture.

Though your group of objects remains the same throughout this exercise, each finished drawing will appear surprisingly different in character and even in composition. This demonstrates an interesting point, namely that the shapes created by the linking patches of tone are just as important compositionally as the actual physical boundaries of the objects.

Fred Dubery,
Kitchen Conversation,
71 x 76 cm (28 x 30 in).
The sharp ellipses of light and the lit surface of the table form a visual counterpoint to the faces of the sitters, which are in shadow. To me, this gives the painting an added psychological dimension – although the figures aren't the most visually assertive element of the composition, our eye is nevertheless drawn to them.

Irises and Ironstone Plate

◀ STEP 1
Having prepared my canvas with an earth-coloured ground, I begin by painting the nearest flower and make a few marks to indicate the rest of the composition. At this stage I am alternating between two brushes: a large flat to lay in the broad masses and a small round hog to make the drawing marks.

◀ STEP 2
I indicate the plate, the edges of the table and the rest of the flowers and make small adjustments to the composition, which is basically a grid of near horizontal and vertical lines. The water in the jar acts like a distorting lens, and I become aware that the 'X' shape created by the iris stems are an important compositional element. Sometimes a subject grabs your attention and you must try to find its essence as you paint rather than working out too much beforehand.

▲ STEP 3
The earth-coloured ground is a bit too obtrusive still and I am anxious to cover most of it up. I concentrate on the inner part of the plate and the blue table top. I've got the shadows around the plate a little too dark but I'll come back to that in a minute. There are shadows running across the table on the right hand side that need some explaining. There are several different blues here, ranging from the greenish Coeruleum of the table top through to the more Ultramarine blue/violet of the iris heads.

▶ STEP 4

Painting the bottles on the right hand side is changing the character of the painting. I'm lightening the shadows to bring the tones closer together and beginning to indicate more of the flower heads and the radiating pattern of the leaves. Using smaller brushes now, I'm working over the whole canvas at once so that the image emerges as a whole rather than as a series of disparate parts. Conscious that some of it is looking a bit 'edgy', I knock back some of the fussy detail with a rag.

◀ STEP 5

The shadow colour on the left hand side is much too warm so that is adjusted next. More detail is added to the plate and the flower heads are given more attention. Throughout the course of the painting I've done much of the work on the palette, mixing up patches of related colours ready for use. I've taken this about as far as I can in one session and ideally would like to make some further adjustments using glazes, but that will have to wait until today's work is dry.

VIEWPOINT AND EYE LEVEL

Having decided what you want to paint you next need to decide where your viewpoint will be and how much to take in. Both these decisions depend on what has excited you about the subject. If your interest is in the textures or patterns of fabrics and natural objects you might want to work up close. From a greater distance you could throw open some cupboard doors and paint the contents ranged on the shelves at various levels, or include a glimpse of the room behind the still-life group.

We are used to looking at our surroundings from normal eye level, so seeing things from a high or low viewpoint is fascinating because it is relatively unfamiliar. Bear this in mind when painting still lifes; an imaginative viewpoint can make for a more striking image. Try looking at the group from low down and you will find that the objects take on a rather monumental appearance as they loom above you. Stand up and view the same group from a higher eye level and you will find that you are much more aware of the table surface and that any round

Viewed from a low eye level, humble objects can take on a feeling of monumentality and make a stable composition.

objects like pots and pans form ellipses that link to form serpentine lines running back into the picture plane. There will be a much stronger sense of the group as a two-dimensional pattern of individual objects seen against the background of the table top.

Roses and Indian Tree,
20 x 25 cm (8 x 10 in).
By looking down on this subject the little roses got tangled up with the pattern on the plate in a way that I enjoyed painting.

MOVING IN CLOSE

There is something about sitting very close to your subject that makes you intensely aware of its physical presence. There are few distractions and you don't necessarily have to worry about creating an illusion of depth and space. The surface qualities of the objects involved take on a greater significance when viewed at this range, and the precise relationships between the objects can be studied with close attention.

Roses,
20 x 22.5 cm (8 x 9 in).
Moving in close on your subject, particularly if it is a single object, can be an absorbing way of working as there are few distractions.

Coolhouse Interior, 91.5 x 81 cm (36 x 32 in). While some compositions fall into place in the first sketch, others evolve less immediately into their final form. This painting of a greenhouse went through several changes before arriving at its present state. Because I started painting in the late afternoon the glazing bars at the top left appeared very dark against the sky. This strong contrast right up in the corner of the painting pulled my eye too much in that direction so I reworked the image, painting early in the morning.

INTERIORS

The first interior that most people paint or draw is often a part of their own home, and there is no shortage of subjects available to you even if you restrict yourself to documenting a single room. Learn to look at your most familiar surroundings with a fresh eye and you'll experience the thrill of rediscovering something that you've probably seen every day and taken for granted. Artists often make paintings of their own studios, for example, providing a fascinating glimpse into their lives.

Away from home there is a wealth of material to be discovered in cafés and restaurants, theatres and concert halls, factories and shops, to name but a few. The interior may simply be a backdrop to the main subject – a still life or portrait, perhaps – but often it is treated as an important subject in its own right.

Fred Dubery,
*Hondecoeter
Mezzotint,*
61 x 51 cm
(24 x 20 in).
The artist has
seized on the
magical
properties of
reflections,
marrying his own
reflected image,
and that of the
room in which he
works, with the
farmyard fowls in
the print.

USING REFLECTIONS

Whether illuminated by natural daylight or
artificial light, the closed environment of a room
provides many possibilities for exploring the
effects of light on composition. Often, for
example, the light source is channelled through
the relatively small area of a window, creating
interesting patterns of light and shadow on
walls and floor.

Reflections in mirrors and windows and on
shiny surfaces can be used to intriguing effect,
both as a way of enlarging the pictorial space
and introducing repeated shapes which tie the
composition together. The painting by Fred
Dubery, above, illustrates very well the way that
reflections can tie images together in mysterious
and unexpected ways.

PERSPECTIVE

The rules of linear perspective apply to interiors
in the same way as they do out of doors. If you
want to tackle a broad sweep in an interior
space, rather than just concentrating on a small
part, I would suggest making a careful
measured drawing first (see page 34) and
choosing a view where the perspective is
relatively straightforward. Begin by establishing
your eye level (see page 78) and relate your
surroundings to that.

Aerial perspective is usually discussed in
relation to landscape, but it plays a part in
interiors, too, especially in a large building like
a cathedral or a railway station. You will find
more information about depicting spatial effects
in the following chapter.

Jane Corsellis,
Beach Reflections,
115 x 127 cm
(45 x 50 in).

COURTESY OF RICHARD
HAGEN LTD

I love the way reflections enable you to introduce intriguing ambiguities that keep the viewer guessing. In this view from a verandah above a tropical beach the artist has managed to convey the feeling that she has paradise to herself, while at the same time the reflection of the beach umbrellas gives the game away.

INSIDE LOOKING OUT

I love painting windows and most of my own paintings of interiors include a glimpse of the outside world. The inclusion of a window or an open doorway adds an extra dimension to the composition by providing a tantalizing glimpse of something outside the room. It arouses our curiosity and stimulates our imagination, and there's a delicious ambiguity about painting from inside looking out.

Compositionally, windows and open doorways create a 'frame within a frame' which can be used to focus attention on the subject of the picture – perhaps a sunlit patch of garden ouside the living room. They also create a sense of continuing space which helps to give depth to the interior itself.

Last but not least, looking out from an interior space gives you the opportunity to explore the contrast between natural light (or darkness) outside and artificial light indoors. I particularly enjoy painting subjects positioned *contre jour* (against the light). A vase of daffodils placed on a sunny windowsill is magically transformed when light shines through the translucent petals from the window behind, so that the blooms are brilliantly lit in contrast with the shadowy tones of the room itself.

INTERIORS WITH FIGURES

Including a figure or figures in an interior scene adds a narrative element that brings it to life, and also provides a standard for scale. The studio interior with model is a genre of painting with a rich history, but other less formal possibilities might include the artist's family and friends, diners in a restaurant or the audience at a concert or play.

Human subjects always attract attention, so you don't necessarily have to feature them in a dominant position within the picture space.

Indeed, if the figure is placed in the middle ground or background it gives the viewer the added pleasure of 'discovery'. If they are incidental to the main subject, figures should be stated in simple terms without too much regard to features or details, otherwise they attract too much attention. Try to paint them with a minimum of brushstrokes, tending towards understatement rather than overstatement in the degree of finish, so that they blend naturally with their surroundings. This is good news, of course, for those painters who are less than confident about painting faces and figures!

Bob Brown, *Morning*, 51 x 61 cm (20 x 24 in). The artist interprets the classical subject of the model in the studio with a definite touch of the exotic.

PROJECT
TABLESCAPE

Medium
Oil paint

Colours
Titanium White, Lemon
Yellow, Cadmium Yellow,
Raw Sienna, Cadmium
Scarlet, Permanent Rose,
French Ultramarine,
Coeruleum Blue, Terre Verte,
Chrome Oxide Green,
Raw Umber

Surface
Prepared canvas or oil
sketching paper

Size
Approximately 41 x 51 cm
(16 x 20 in)

Equipment
A selection of round and
filbert hog bristle brushes in
a range of sizes
Turpentine
Oil-painting medium
Palette
Dipper
Palette knife
Easel

Time
1-3 hours for each painting

▼ Two lamps here create a sequence of 'light-dark-light-dark' and objects are seen either brightly lit or steeped in shadow. Although this lighting set-up has been deliberately arranged, it is similar to the lighting found in many rooms and not unlike some aspects of light in the landscape.

In my own work, I am often struck by the extent to which ideas and qualities are sometimes carried over between the seemingly disparate categories of landscape and still life. This is partly due to the way that I use light, often using backlighting, either from studio lamps or the sun, but the inclusion of plants and flowers as well as the of the view through a window to the outdoors itself adds to this blurring of distinctions, which can lead to a fresh approach.

By spreading objects out across a large table and lighting to create 'puddles' of light and shadow you can create a situation as much like a sort of indoor landscape as it is like conventional still life. This is a good subject to try out in the evening or on a dull day, when the artificial light will not be swamped by daylight flooding in from outside.

A low eye level will emphasize the effect more and give an interesting counterchange between light and dark areas. Try using paint straight away without any preliminary drawing, perhaps using a restricted palette for the first one or two studies.

Studio Table,
51 x 45 cm (20 x 18 in).
One of the tables in my
studio. The starting point for
this painting was the roses
silhouetted against the bright
light reflecting off the glass
on the framed picture at the
back. Most of the ingredients
of this painting were already
in place, but I moved one or
two things around a little in
the interests of making a
better composition.

▼ Using a larger table and
more light sources will create
a more complex effect.

SELF-ASSESSMENT

✧ Have you created a
feeling of space and
three-dimensional form
through your use of light?

✧ Did you use
counterchange (the
contrast of light against
dark, dark against light)
to set up visual rhythms
that lead the eye around
the composition?

✧ Have you managed
accurately to reproduce
the tones that you can
see, or are some of the
darks a bit too dark?

CHAPTER EIGHT

SPACE & PERSPECTIVE

Over the centuries artists have developed various means of creating the illusion of space and recession within a painting. Some of these have been emphasized more than others by western art, and many student painters see perspective, with all its potential difficulties, as the only proper way to depict three-dimensional space. Well, of course it isn't, though it is useful to know the basic principles.

The inclusion of tonal and colour contrasts, converging lines, overlapping forms and diminishing scale are just some of the compositional devices that can be used alongside formal perspective to subtly suggest a three-dimensional world within the confines of the picture frame.

Different subjects may call for different means of depicting space. In a landscape scene, for example, there may not be much need to worry about formal linear perspective, but a grasp of aerial perspective and diminishing scale will be absolutely essential. The illusion of space will be heightened if a number of these methods are used together, but for the purposes of this chapter we'll look at them one at a time.

▶ Jane Corsellis,
*Villa Pardini,
Lucca,*
35.5 x 20.5 cm
(14 x 8 in)

Dorset Sky,
25.5 x 30.5 cm
(10 x 12 in).
In the evening, when failing light begins to simplify things, it is often easier to get a feel for space and scale. You don't have to paint large pictures to express a feeling of the vastness of the landscape.

Beach Family and Racing Cats, Bénodet, 23 x 30.5 cm (9 x 12 in). I love the 'layered' effect you often get when looking across a beach to the sea. The sky, right at the back, is overlaid by the sails of the boats, while the foreground figures break up the horizontal line of the rocks.

USING SCALE

Even without an understanding of the intricacies of geometric perspective it is easy to grasp that things close to us appear larger than those further away. By using these changes in scale as a means of establishing foreground, middle ground and background, we can begin to create quite a strong impression of receding space in our pictures.

Curiously, our eyes often mislead us into reducing the size of nearby objects and increasing the size of things in the distance. I think this 'telescope' effect is a result of the brain discounting information from the eye, preferring to rely on its own knowledge that size is constant.

OVERLAPPING FORMS

Another effective way of creating the illusion of three-dimensional space is by overlapping elements in a picture. When two shapes overlap,

the eye perceives one as being behind the other and therefore further from the eye. Even when the objects are of the same size, the eye tends to accept a condition of depth when one overlaps the other.

This simple point is often overlooked by inexperienced painters. If two objects are placed on the same visual plane a degree of ambiguity is set up which lessens the impression of space and distance.

AERIAL PERSPECTIVE

The most important means of establishing the illusion of space and atmosphere in landscape compostions, and sometimes in interior scenes too, is through aerial perspective. The term 'aerial perspective' (sometimes called 'atmospheric perspective') describes a phenomenon which you have no doubt noticed when painting in the open air; objects which are far off in the distance appear hazier, bluer and lighter in tone than those closer to us. This is an optical illusion caused by the presence of water vapour and particles of dust in the atmosphere. The effect is more apparent on misty days than when the air is very clear but the effect is always there.

Tones appear strongest in the foreground, becoming progressively weaker in the distance. Full light and dark is most obvious in the near foreground, the contrast between these extremes becoming progressively weaker in the distance.

Together with the reduction in tonal contrast there is a colour shift as the atmosphere filters out red light from distant objects, giving distant hills and trees a bluish tinge. Once again this effect is most noticeable when large distances are involved.

Inexperienced painters sometimes tend to paint the distant landscape with too much detail and clarity and with strong colours. This is because they have fallen into the trap of painting what they know, instead of what they see; they 'know' a tree is green, so they paint it green, even though it is on the horizon and actually appears blue.

A view from my favourite hilltop on a hazy day. Notice how the strongest contrasts of tone are in the foreground, becoming closer together as you approach the horizon.

▶ With more intervening atmosphere absorbing light from the red end of the spectrum, colour becomes shifted towards blue as you approach the horizon and colour contrasts in general are reduced.

LINEAR PERSPECTIVE

Far from being the daunting thing most people think it is, linear perspective is really very simple, and no doubt you have a fairly good grasp of it already. Basically, it all hinges on the fact that parallel horizontal lines seen receding into the distance appear to converge at a single point on the horizon.

HORIZON LINE

Before you can draw anything in perspective you must first establish the horizon line, which always corresponds with your eye level. A simple experiment will demonstrate this. Sit down and look out of a window and notice at what point the horizon cuts across the window frame. Now stand up, and observe how the horizon rises up with you. If your view of the horizon is obscured by trees or buildings, hold a pencil horizontally in front of your eyes and note where it cuts across the scene.

VANISHING POINTS

The point on the horizon line at which receding parallel lines appear to converge is the vanishing point. Depending on the position of the subject in relation to the artist, there might be one, two, or even several vanishing points in one picture.

ONE-POINT PERSPECTIVE

If you are looking at a subject directly in line with your line of vision (say you are standing in the middle of a long, straight road) then all receding parallel lines will appear to converge at dead centre – the point on the horizon line that coincides with your centre of vision. All lines above your eye level, such as telegraph wires, will move down to the vanishing point; all lines below your eye level, such as the edges of the road, will move up to the vanishing point. This is the simplest form of perspective.

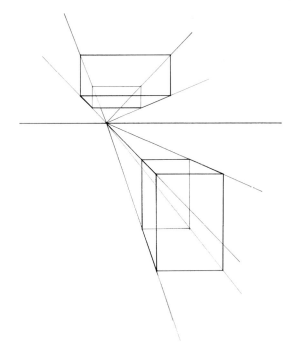

▲ One-point perspective. There is just one vanishing point on your eye level for all of these boxes because they are all parallel with your centre of vision.

▼ I have slightly simplified this view to make it all relate to one vanishing point. When looking down from a high viewpoint your eyel level is correspondingly high.

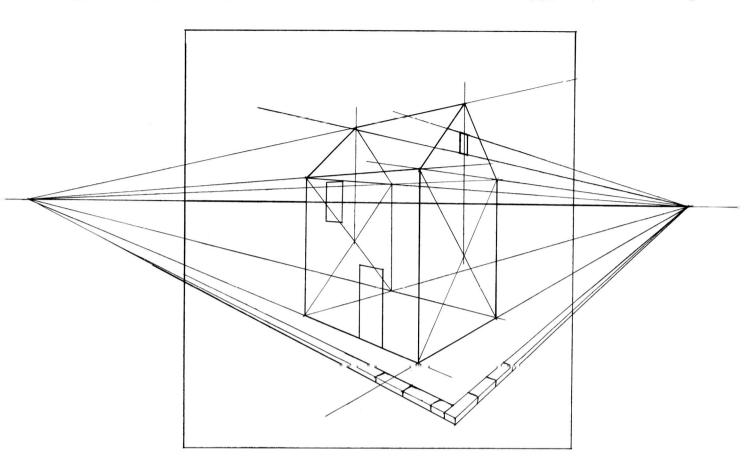

TWO-POINT PERSPECTIVE

If you stand on a street corner so that you can see two sides of the building opposite, you have two-point perspective: the visible sides both have converging lines and these meet at two separate vanishing points, one on either side of the building. This time, neither vanishing point coincides with your centre of vision.

When two-point perspective is involved, it is likely that at least one vanishing point, and sometimes both, will be outside the picture area. You have to imagine the vanishing points in the space beyond your support and estimate the angles of buildings and so on by eye.

Two-point perspective applies in situations where the subject is viewed from an oblique angle. Two vanishing points can be located on the horizon line.

EXERCISE

Raid the kitchen cupboards for anything in boxes and place them on a table so that they are arranged square with the table top and parallel to each other. Position yourself so that your line of sight is square on to the table and make a drawing of what you see. Now light the group strongly from above and to one side and make drawn or painted sketches. Check that the perspective is correct and that the boxes appear solid and three-dimensional.

CHAPTER NINE

LANDSCAPES & SEASCAPES

Without doubt the most popular painting subject of all is landscape. For this reason we are perhaps conditioned to seeing landscape subjects through the eyes of other painters, past and present, and so we must work that bit harder to look at this theme with fresh eyes.

Landscape is a wonderfully rich resource for painters and extends far beyond the pastoral idyll. When you are out painting on location, be ready to see small subjects as well as large ones. And while you're working on one painting, look for further possibilities to paint another day. My diary is full of such notes, reminding me that the sun will rise at a particular spot on a certain day in spring, or to go back to look at an interesting view at dusk.

For those of us who paint regularly, the activity itself quickly takes over and becomes more absorbing than the detail of making a particular painting. Once you find a subject that you're in sympathy with, the images you make will seem to learn from each other and in this way your painting style develops and is enriched by your experiences.

▶ *South from Eggardon*, 76 x 71 cm (30 x 24 in). The site in this painting is an Iron Age hill fort some miles inland. The view to the sea draws one's eye up towards the horizon, which is why I chose to use a portrait-format canvas.

Jacqueline Rizvi, *Iceland, Plain and Mountains*, 71 x 91 cm (28 x 36 in). The artist's response to the unfamiliar. She writes: "The landscape forms are typical - a flat plain of volcanic grit on which nothing grows except grey/green moss ... mountains very abrupt, no soft foothills."

APPROACHING THE SUBJECT

In my experience the 'grand view' rarely makes a good painting. Grand views are nearly always about middle distance and far distance and ironically, if there is little happening in the foreground, they can lack a feeling of depth and space. Creating a sense of the landscape rolling back to a horizon which may be many miles away is also technically very demanding. To

▲ *Portland and Chesil,*
14 x 30.5 cm (5½ x 12 in).
This is a small painting and even then had to be painted quickly. When I started the sun was to the left but as I worked it moved further to the right and the glare of light on the sea altered the view completely.

▼ *Snow and Sea,*
West Dorset,
13 x 30.5 cm (5 x 12 in).
For me, snow is a compelling subject and if it only lasts a few days I'm full of nervous energy trying to make the most of it. The subject here is the snow-covered hills backlit by the glare from the sea.

begin with at least, you should tackle smaller, more intimate subjects. Frequently, the most simple, everyday scenes make the best paintings. It isn't difficult to find something to paint and, of course, it is the way the artist sees and interprets the subject that makes for interesting pictures.

Remember, too, that the sun is constantly on the move. It will make shadows revolve around trees and suddenly plunge the lit side of a hill into the shade. Diligently painting on regardless of these sorts of changes can lead to a muddled and contradictory picture. A day's painting may be better spent producing two or three small paintings than struggling on with one big one.

If you do like to work on a large scale you have the option of making small studies and

West from Eggardon, 25.5 x 30.5 cm (10 x 12 in). I paint this valley a lot. There's usually the distraction of deer and buzzards but the constantly changing pattern of the fields and the weather seen from this height make it a favourite starting spot for a day's work.

sketches on location and using these as the basis for a studio painting. Alternatively, and providing you have a settled spell of weather, you could do as Monet did and return to the same spot over several days, always working at the same time of day and painting for no more than two or three hours at a time. After several days' painting the surface of the painting may become rather sticky and unworkable and will need to be 'rested' for a while, until it is thoroughly dry, before continuing any further.

LANDSCAPE COMPOSITION

Very often landscape subjects will seem to be based on an underlying grid of horizontals and verticals. Bands of cloud, the lines of distant fields and the horizon itself will all tend to be horizontal or nearly so. Against this you have strong vertical accents provided by trees, figures, buildings and so on. Compositions exploiting this grid result in calm, stable paintings and the effect of the grid may be to heighten the viewer's awareness of the picture plane itself.

A more dynamic quality will be found in paintings where the artist has looked for strong diagonals and curving lines which seem to sweep or slice back into the picture plane. These compositions will have a strong sense of space and depth.

CHOOSING THE BEST VIEWPOINT

When considering the composition of your landscape picture it is important to choose your viewpoint with care. Sometimes, because of the way the ground falls away from you, the foreground of your subject can appear to detach itself from the middle distance, or there will be a very strong horizontal element that prevents your eye from travelling smoothly back into the distance. Try also to avoid situations where your

▼ *Light Snowfall, Near Powerstock,* 15 x 30 cm (6 x 12 in). Early morning with a dusting of overnight snow. The winter bareness of the trees makes this a much better subject than it is in the summer when the houses are invisible.

attention is divided between two equally strong features at either side of your composition as this creates a sort of 'ding-dong' effect, with your eye bouncing back and forth from one side of the painting to the other like a spectator at a tennis match.

Beyond this advice and your own sensitivity to what 'works' I won't say too much about composition as I think too much writing on the subject promotes the fiction that there are perfect compositions out there and all we have to do is find them. In reality, each painting situation will be different to the next and you have to work with what's in front of you.

Neither would I advocate moving things around. If you choose to ignore a tree you have to fill its space with something else. Nature tends to put the elements of landscape together in a way that has an inherent rightness that we painters cannot invent. You can do so much simply by choosing your viewpoint with care that further invention isn't really necessary. In my view, the only important compositional rule is 'if it looks right, it is right'.

Jane Corsellis,
Estuary (January),
51 x 152.5 cm (20 x 60 in).

IN THE COLLECTION OF
FRESHFIELDS
This wonderful, spacious composition takes its cue from the natural shape of the widening river. Though there is a lot of 'empty' space in the picture it is nevertherless full of interest and the patterns on the water subtly lead the eye back in space.

EXERCISE

Make small paintings on oil sketching paper as a way of discovering the boundaries and proportions of a potential painting subject. Start near the centre of the sheet with what interests you most and gradually work your way out until the limits of the idea seem to have been reached. On your return home, use strips of card to 'frame' your sketch along the boundaries that you've arrived at to see if this confirms what you've found, and then experiment with other framing possibilities.

PROJECT
FINDING A VIEW

Medium
Oil paint

Colours
Titanium White, Lemon Yellow, Cadmium Yellow, Raw Sienna, Cadmium Scarlet, Permanent Rose, French Ultramarine, Coeruleum Blue, Terre Verte, Chrome Oxide Green, Raw Umber

Surfaces
Sketchbook
Prepared painting boards

Size
Approximately 20 x 25 cm
(8 x 10 in)

Equipment
Your outdoor painting kit
and drawing materials

Time
Approximately 10 minutes
for each sketch, an hour for
each painting

▼ The location for all of these studies is a bend in the River Loire with an island in mid river. This aspect of the subject, looking along the river into the light, was enormously attractive but I needed to know how much to include. The viewfinder told me how important the tree on the extreme right was, acting as a brake to the sweeping diagonals leading out of the picture.

Walking around a new location looking for potential subjects can be an exciting business and often several compositional choices can compete for your attention. Using a viewfinder (as described on page 38) is an excellent way of assessing the various possibilities and deciding which to tackle first.

Next time you find yourself painting in unfamiliar territory, if you have time, start by taking a walk round with your sketchbook and a viewfinder, and note down anything that really grabs your attention. From any one position there may be several directions of view that offer subjects for painting, and within each view there may be several aspects that tempt you to explore

further. Bring the viewfinder closer to your eye to include a wide-angle view, push it away from you to select a narrow one. When you've found several views that you really want to paint, your only problem is deciding which to paint first!

Good compositions depend to a large extent on the relationships between the shapes within the painting and its edges, but landscape subjects tend not to have clearly defined edges; a viewfinder will help you see more easily how the shapes of the composition lock together. As an added bonus the black of the card can be a useful reference when making tonal judgements and will help to stop you pitching the darkest tones too dark.

This illustration shows a wide-angle view of the same location, within which the coloured lines enclose rectangles that could offer further compositions by including only part of the view. The bankside vegetation in the foreground could be very useful as a 'scale-setter' if I want to stress the dramatic feeling of depth as the river sweeps back towards the horizon.

◀ This drawing homes in on the island, with the trees and grazing cattle silhouetted against the bright water beyond. This scene is different in character from the first two studies, although I drew all three without moving my feet. The previous studies were about space and perspective whereas this one offers the subject in frieze-like bands across the picture plane.

◀ Taking a narrow view looking down the river offered delicious high-key colour and a feeling of great distance and a big sky. A very quick oil sketch helps me to remember the atmosphere of the place and will draw me back for a longer visit.

SELF-ASSESSMENT

✧ How many different compositions could you find at your chosen locations?

✧ What difference would time of day and lighting make to your selection of a particular view?

✧ Has the viewfinder helped you accurately to gauge the relative scale of different parts of the scene, with the foreground big enough and the background small enough?

A SENSE OF WHOLENESS

Although I am very keen to blur the somewhat artificial divisions between various categories of painting, even I have to acknowledge that landscape is different from other subjects in one important respect. Landscape is so often about space, the sensation of light and above all about spirit of place, rather than with the cold representation of detail.

It is important to remember that you are painting a particular instant as well as a particular place. Novice painters are often concerned about their work depicting a certain place, but don't give any thought to the unity of image that comes from looking at the sky, the land mass and the direction and quality of light as all part of the same process. For example, if you look at the landscape on a sunny summer day with the light coming from one side, the round forms of the trees is likely to be echoed by the roundness of the clouds above them. Turn through ninety degrees so that the light comes from directly behind you and all parts of the composition will appear to be flattened by this frontal lighting. Turn around so you are looking into the sun and the trees and clouds

Morning Trees, Dinton,
13 x 23 cm (5 x 9 in).
Painted early in the morning,
before breakfast and a day's
teaching. The sun had risen
behind me and was shining
full onto the trees on the
hillside ahead. I particularly
enjoyed the sensation of their
bare green trunks against
the flashes of blue of the sky
beyond.

are likely to be rim lit in a similar way. By being sensitive to these connections you will establish a sense of unity in your painting that will tell you about that particular place at a particular time of day.

RESPONDING TO LIGHT

You can't paint landscape regularly without developing a sensitivity to light. The veiled quality of the sun gleaming through low cloud or the peculiar intensity of colour after a spring shower have a heightened significance when you've struggled to catch such fleeting effects in paint. The solidity and timelessness of the underlying bones of the landscape are a foil to the momentary effects of the passage of light,

and part of the thrill of painting landscape lies in trying to reconcile these very different perceptions.

A single location can take on a very different aspect depending on the weather and the time of day. At dawn and dusk you have a short period when you can work with the sun below the horizon and explore the particular quality of this rather directionless, reflected light. At times, often after a period of squally rain, the sky will break up into rags and tatters, allowing the sun to shine through the gaps in the cloud like a sweeping spotlight. At such times I know there will be exciting subjects to be found, providing I work small enough to be adaptable and make changes as the scene unfolds. It is at times like this that oil paint really comes into its own.

Lambert's Castle, 61 x 91.5 cm (24 x 36 in). Snow again. The study for this was painted by the road, under trees laden with hoar frost. The light in the shadowy foreground had a strong blue tinge while the background trees, lit by the hazy sunshine, were quite orangey. This curious reversal of the normal rules of aerial perspective shows that you must always be prepared for the unexpected.

Landscape
in Changeable Light

▲ 2

▼ 3

▲ STEP 1

Looking out from the top of a hill with a breeze blowing towards me, alternating bands of sunshine and shadow are slowly crossing the landscape. As I start to work, the whole of the foreground, including the village, is in shadow, while the distant sunlit hills are all cool blues, blue-greens and violets. Using a large flat hog brush, I quickly block in the whole composition, having previously spent some time mixing 'puddles' of colour on my palette.

STEP 2

I now start to indicate the hedges and fields. Already the diminishing scale of the fields is beginning to heighten the sense of spatial recession. From this viewpoint the hedgelines make a broad zig-zag, taking the eye back into the picture. The subtle diagonal tilt of the nearest hedge is really helping; a stricter horizontal line here would tend to stop the eye travelling back into the distance.

STEP 3

The moving clouds have opened up and the village in the foreground is now strongly lit. It takes very little time to re-state the foreground with broad brush strokes. It is important to be prepared to make changes throughout the time it takes to make a painting. It's always easier than you expect, and far easier than trying to remember the scene as it was. If it all changes too fast, start another painting.

STEP 4
The changes in the lighting are happening less quickly now so I snatch time to consolidate the drawing and add detail in the middle distance before moving up to the horizon and indicating the hill on the left. I also adjust the tones at the horizon, bringing them closer together.

STEP 5
Turning my attention to the sky, I find that the pinkish imprimatura showing through the overlaid colours mimics closely the feeling of warmth behind the cooler colours of the sky. Always grateful for happy accidents, I leave some of this colour untouched but structure the sky a little more.

Dinghies and Watchers, Bénodet,
15 x 20 cm (6 x 8 in).
I'd spent the morning painting on this beach in Brittany and had already started on this little picture when several people stood up and began keenly watching the racing dinghies.

SEASCAPES

I am lucky in living near the sea and a large proportion of my work is about the local beaches and harbours. But even for the occasional visitor, the sea coast offers a wealth of inspiration.

Not many of my paintings are portraits of the sea itself, though this can be done very beautifully and many haunting images consisting of nothing but sea and sky have been painted. I interpret seascape to include all the bustling, busy subjects along the shoreline and in ports and harbours. For me the biggest appeal of seascapes lies in the constant movement and variety they present, in all seasons and all weathers.

Beaches are wonderful places to paint once you have overcome any nerves about working in so public a place. The hardest bit is getting

Weymouth Harbour, Evening,
20 x 25.5 cm (8 x 10 in).
This was painted in a rapidly darkening dusk with barely enough light to work by. Painting the sea, whether it's open ocean or harbour, you've always got to cope with the element of change and the need to get it done today, because it will look quite different tomorrow.

started, but I usually find that once I've set up my easel and squeezed out some colour the excitement of the subject tends to take over. If you work discreetly, sitting with a pochade box on your lap, it is surprising how little notice people will take of you. Sitting down, preferably with your back against something solid, curious passers by can't stare over your shoulder!

Beaches give you an opportunity to study people at close quarters when they are at their most relaxed, and once a family have staked their territory they often stay all day.

Bo Hilton,
Windbreak,
51 x 61 cm (20 x 24 in).
The artist concentrates here on the brilliantly coloured, abstract patterns of light shining through the windbreak, contrasting with the near silhouettes of the children in front.

FORWARD PLANNING

A little thought and planning before you start painting is well worthwhile. If you intend working for a whole day by the sea, make sure you have some means of protecting finished paintings from kicked sand. You need to be able to clean your palette and dipper from time to time so take along some plastic bags and bottles to put your waste rags and turpentine in so that you can dispose of them responsibly later. Think too about what you will wear; it's important that you feel comfortable and blend in with the holidaymakers. A large-brimmed hat to keep the sun out of your eyes is a must. Sunglasses

Topsham,
91.5 x 101.5 cm
(36 x 40 in).
This is one of a series of paintings I made using on-the-spot sketches. I liked the view from this high vantage point. The masts of the boats link the foreground with the high, distant horizon while the perspective of their shadows acts as a counter to the strong diagonal of the quayside.

Mary Jackson,
The Pier at Eastbourne,
61 x 51 cm (24 x 20 in).
The pier at low tide, with the distant surf glimpsed through its 'legs', makes an interesting subject. Notice how the figures on the pier itself give a sense of scale to the picture.

may be of some help when you are trying to identify where the brightest tones are.

You will be painting in a very fluid situation and compositions will often tend to evolve rather than being planned at the outset, so think carefully about what type of surface you are going to work on. Ready-made canvases may be somewhat inflexible in proportion to enable you to fine tune a composition, whereas you can start and finish anywhere on a board or a pad of oil sketching paper, and trim or centre later. Canvases, too, being very light, are easily blown about and on a beach or by the water this could be disastrous. It makes sense to keep your paintings small, on a scale that you can realistically complete in one session.

CHAPTER TEN

TOWNSCAPES

Diners and Salute,
30.5 x 51 cm
(12 x 20 in).
For the pigeons in
Venice it's
lunchtime all day.
I liked the contrast
of the brightly
coloured
sunshades and
tables against the
quieter greys
elsewhere.

Considering that the majority of people today live in towns and cities, urban scenes rank surprisingly low in popularity as a painting theme. Yet streets and buildings are marvellous subjects, endlessly varied and offering plenty of scope for exciting interpretation. And the venue doesn't have to be Venice, Rome or Paris; an ordinary suburban street can offer just as many possibilities.

The thought of painting in a busy street in full view of people can be nerve-racking at first. But I find that once you get started it is easier than you expect and, on the whole, people let you work undisturbed. It is essential to keep your painting equipment lightweight and compact so that you can work discreetly without getting in everyone's way. I find a little pochade box most convenient and one can appear unobtrusive tucked away in a quiet corner. And if it really is impractical to work on-the-spot in oils you can usually slip into a doorway to make reference sketches.

▶ Tom Coates,
Parisian Street,
51 x 41 cm
(20 x 16 in).
The street-level
activity of people
and cars is
played off against
the static,
interlocking
shapes of
buildings and sky
in this beautiful
painting.

◀ *By the Accademia, Venice*, 92 x 102 cm (36 x 40 in). The pattern of the large, sunlit architectural blocks forms the backdrop to this painting of the busy little space at the foot of the Accademia Bridge.

▶ Bob Brown, *A Helping Hand, Chartres*, 91.5 x 119.5 cm (36 x 47 in). The three big arches have an almost abstract grandeur but the tiny figures are vital in establishing the dramatic scale of the building. The 'lost and found' quality of the figures acknowledges that the people are just a fleeting incident compared with the permanence of the great cathedral.

START SIMPLY

It is best to avoid very ambitious projects initially as it is easy to become discouraged if your first attempts fail. Choose a small corner, something with simple perspective; a small architectural detail or a single façade can be just as fascinating as a sweeping panorama. If you find the right vantage point you can position yourself square on to a building and use its façade as a backdrop to the activity in the street. Often the contour of a building will be broken up by trees and shadows or passing traffic and this will enable you to concentrate on the subject's painterly qualities without getting too preoccupied with the intricacies of the drawing.

COPING WITH PERSPECTIVE

Until you are fully familiar with some of the refinements of perspective, urban settings that rely heavily on the accurate drawing of large

A drawing from my Venice sketchbook, intended as a working drawing for a painting. I used the horizontals and verticals of the building as a grid to scale the foreground by. I drew from a standing position so all the heads are at eye level.

buildings may seem rather daunting. But while the rules of perspective will help you to understand and interpret what you see, it is important to look first. The comparative measuring techniques described on page 34 can be used together with the simple rules of perspective to refine your first impressions and give your painting a sense of solidity.

Streets and buildings may appear complicated at first because they are covered in all sorts of detail; chimneys, doors, windows, balconies and so on. However, beneath all that artifice, most buildings are basically made up of a series of cubes of varying size – and if you can draw a cube in perspective you can certainly draw a building.

Once you are confident about using perspective you have the choice of working from ground level or finding a position higher up which allows you to look out over the roof tops for a more panoramic view.

ESTABLISHING SCALE

When you paint streets and buildings, bear in mind the need to establish a sense of scale. It is difficult to judge the intended scale of objects in a picture except by association. A painting of a grand cathedral, for instance, may lack impact if there is nothing else in the picture to use as a point of comparison. Figures make the best 'scale setters'; since we know what size they really are, it is easy to get an idea of the size of a building in relation to them. In the painting of Chartres Cathedral by Bob Brown (above) the great cliff of the façade is emphasized by the tiny figures.

A sketchbook allows you to 'rehearse' a new subject and try out compositions.

EXERCISES

1 On a walk around town make a sequence of sketchbook drawings exploring the major compositional shapes and the way that they interlock. Many views along streets will give you just three or four major shapes, including perhaps the shape of the sky against the rooftops of buildings. This exercise will encourage you to see potential paintings in terms of their main compositional elements.

2 Towns are texturally very rich. Make some painted studies which focus in on different qualities of surface. You might look at crumbling brick, glass, wet roads, shiny chrome and vegetation and how these come together in particular views.

ON-THE-SPOT SKETCHES

Often it is difficult to see potential painting subjects simply because we take our familiar surroundings for granted, and we are all so accustomed to walking or driving through towns that to stand and look is a novel experience. I would suggest you go for a slow walk with your trusty viewfinder, a small sketchbook and a pocket full of pencils and see what you can find. If you want to capture the spirit of a place there is no better way than by making on-the-spot sketches. While you are sketching you are unconsciously absorbing the sounds, the smells, the 'flavour' of the place.

Work without drawing too much attention to yourself and the chances are that no-one will take any notice of you, they're all much too preoccupied with their own business. There are many potential vantage points where you can sit or stand, away from the madding crowd, and draw at your leisure. If all else fails, take refuge inside your car!

LIGHT AND WEATHER

Changing weather conditions and the light at different times of the day can establish atmosphere and mood in your townscapes and transfigure even the most mundane subject. In fine weather tonal effects of light and shade can be explored, with large blocks of shadow cast by buildings cutting across brightly lit streets. Painting early in the morning or late in the afternoon also allows full use of the play of shadows and reflected light.

The misty, diffused light of early evening conveys a quiet mood, and this is the time of day when painting into the light produces memorable effects. Backlit shapes become resolved into single blocks of close tone and figurative details are often lit up around the edge by a 'halo' of shimmering light. Similarly, townscapes made ethereal and insubstantial by fog gain a magical quality.

Bad weather shouldn't be too much of a handicap when working in towns and cities as

Shoppers in Venice, 23 x 36 cm (9 x 14 in). The inspiration for this little painting was the wonderful patterns created by the interplay of natural light and coloured neon, and the reflections in the windows.

there are plenty of places where you can find shelter from the rain. And rainy streets are particularly evocative, especially at night when the bright neon lights of shops and cars are reflected on roads and pavements. Even on the dullest winter's day the bright lights and bustling crowds of an urban shopping centre offer possibilities for the painter that may be hard to find elsewhere. Seek out subjects that you can explore in all weathers. If you restrict your painting only to sunny days you will miss out on some wonderful, subtle effects.

Bath Reflections, 18 x 30.5 cm (7 x 12 in). It had been raining all day and the reflections from the wet pavement combined with those in the windows to create a wonderful patchwork of light and dark shapes. Reflected images in windows and on wet streets are an exciting visual characteristic of city life.

Colleoni Memorial, Venice

▲ 2

▼ 3

▲ STEP 1
I have an entire sketchbook filled with drawings of Venice. This drawing, made on the spot, was one of several pages of studies featuring the Colleoni Memorial. I liked the juxtaposition of the majestic statue with the diminutive man and dog.

STEP 2
I choose a canvas in the same proportions as the drawing and prepare it with an ochre imprimatura. I square up the drawing (see page 36) and transfer the

design to the canvas using charcoal. This is lightly fixed and then further strengthened with drawing marks made with thin oil colour.

STEP 3
The initial blocking in needs to be done quite quickly to establish the broad tonal masses of the composition. The paint is thin enough at this stage to allow the drawing marks to show through, so I can work broadly without worrying too much about obliterating the drawing. The main compositional point of the

painting is established at this stage in the relationship of the man and dog to the giant bronze horseman, and the perspective of the shadows.

STEP 4
I've realized that in my original drawing I've made the figure of the horse a bit too big, so with the aid of another reference drawing I make some adjustments. The red outline allows me to see my revisions clearly. I now spend some time working up the architectural background in more detail and pulling the tones together.

STEP 5
I've tidied up the bronze horse and rider and most of my red revisions have disappeared under new paint. The great marble plinth gets a bit more attention at this stage and I work the sky further to try to keep it integrated with the rest of the painting. I'm pleased that the horse no longer appears to be falling off the front of the plinth!

▲ 4   ▼ 5

SOURCES OF INSPIRATION

You don't have to look hard to find aspects of urban life that will excite you and urge you to paint. It may be the perspective of massive, interlocking blocks of buildings that interests you, or the contrast between grimy buildings and bright neon lights. It might be the theatrical aspect of streets, parks and squares as a setting for people's lives, or the intimate nature of individual doorways or balconies. On the following pages you will find just some of the aspects of painting urban subjects that you might like to consider.

MAN AND NATURE

Much of the appeal of urban subjects lies in the potential for exploiting interesting contrasts and juxtapositions. For example, towns and cities are by definition man-made structures built of concrete and brick. But contained within them are many of the natural elements that form part of the rural environment. Most cities have squares, parks or tree-lined avenues and the contrast of these green spaces nestled among buildings makes a rewarding area of study. And if your viewpoint includes a glimpse of sky, all the better because you can echo the organic forms of the trees in the shapes of the clouds.

ANCIENT AND MODERN

Because of the way in which cities have evolved gradually, often over many centuries, ancient and modern facets of city life often stand side by side, providing another fascinating area of contrast. Ancient churches and castles often stand surrounded by the more humdrum trappings of the twentieth century. Shiny new office blocks stand cheek-by-jowl with dilapidated old warehouses. Brashly coloured shops and awnings contrast with the mellow tones of old brick and stone edifices.

Cities and towns are changing increasingly fast, and it is no exaggeration to say that there is

Tom Coates,
Bridge at Cahors,
51 x 61 cm (20 x 24 in).
This massive stone bridge makes an almost heroic subject, but look again at the delicacy with which the artist plays off the big two-dimensional shapes of sky, bridge and water against their three-dimensional form.

Jane Corsellis,
Summer, Hyde Park,
81.5 x 91.5 cm (32 x 36 in).
People relaxing in the warm
sun by the water – a very
French subject in a very
English setting.

a very real role for the artist as documenter of
the disappearing scene.

THE HUMAN ELEMENT

Amateur painters sometimes shy away from
including figures in their townscapes if they feel
they are not competent enough at figure
painting. But towns and cities are the habitat of
people, so they are an important element in
most urban scenes. Figures bring a street scene
to life and give an indication of the scale of the
surrounding features. Besides, by excluding
them you miss out on the opportunity to exploit
the fascinating contrast between the
permanence and solidity of buildings and the
moving patterns of people and traffic.

People are transitory elements of the scene
compared with the permanence of streets and
buildings, so you have to find appropriate ways
of portraying them. Figures – particularly those

in the distance – should be stated quite loosely
with a few well-placed flicks and dashes of
paint rather than lots of fiddly detail (though
one should observe carefully the action and
attitude of the figure and never resort to using
a slick 'shorthand'). As a rule, photographs are
not a good reference source as they freeze the
movement in a way that appears static and
unnatural.

It can be instructive to carry a sketchbook and
try to record groups of people – stopping to
talk, sitting in a café, waiting in line for a bus.
Work rapidly, drawing and redrawing the
shapes and masses as they move. Rather than
depicting a series of individuals, try to see the
way that knots and groups of people fit
together. If you need more practice at drawing
moving figures, try working at home, drawing
your family and friends as they move, without
asking them to adopt a fixed pose.

Mary Jackson, *Au Vieux Honfleur*, 40.5 x 51 cm (16 x 20 in). An attentive waiter is an important compositional ingredient in this evocative painting. Notice how the artist has kept the paint thin in the shadows, allowing the underpainting to show through, while the paint in the lighter areas is quite thick and buttery.

CAFES AND BARS

Great places for discreetly observing people at ease, cafés and bars have long provided artists with subjects, all the way from the opulence of Florian's in Venice to the local 'greasy spoon'.

STREET MARKETS

The gaiety, colour and movement of street markets make them a tailor-made subject for painting. In a unique way they combine aspects of every painting subject – landscape, buildings, figures and still life. The hustle and bustle of markets may make it difficult to complete a painting on the spot, but armed with a sketchbook and some watercolour paints or coloured pencils you should be able to glean enough reference material to make several paintings back at the studio.

PARKS AND GARDENS

The green spaces of parks and ornamental gardens provide the opportunity to work in relative peace and with space to set up an easel.

They often feature glasshouses and conservatories, ponds, ornamental aviaries and so on which provide a refreshing contrast with their urban surroundings. In fine weather, parks attract many people to relax or eat an informal lunch. Find a suitable viewpoint where you can observe without being disturbed and wait for your subject to come to you.

PAINTING INDOORS

Large public buildings such as churches, museums, railway stations, shops and restaurants offer a rich seam of visual imagery for the painter. The authorities responsible for public buildings will normally be happy for you to paint on the spot provided you don't inconvenience others.

LOOKING OUT OR LOOKING IN

Once inside, your choice of viewpoint could include not just the interior itself but also a view through a door to a room beyond, or onto the street outside. Interior subjects that include a view through to the outside world have a particular fascination for me because it creates an intriguing double image – a frame within a frame. The success of such images depends on pitching the tones just right; the natural daylight outside is probably much brighter than that inside the building.

A reversal of the same theme – looking into a dimly lit interior from a bright street – also makes for interesting pictures. Again, watch your tones carefully, and use colourful darks in the interior otherwise it will simply create a black hole in your painting.

▼ Jane Corsellis,
Winter, Kensington Gardens,
81.5 x 91.5 cm (32 x 36 in).
A lovely, restrained painting with soft winter sunshine picking out the tracery of trees and railings. In the city, parks and gardens provide a sort of outdoor theatre throughout the year.

▶ Mary Jackson,
The Balcony,
36 x 25.5 cm (14 x 10 in).
The view in through the window is intriguing and adds an extra dimension to this façade. Notice how the artist has found rich colour within the dark tones of the interior.

PROJECT
FINDING STREET SUBJECTS

✧

Medium
Oil paint

✧

Colours
Titanium White, Lemon
Yellow, Cadmium Yellow,
Raw Sienna, Cadmium
Scarlet, Permanent Rose,
French Ultramarine,
Coeruleum Blue, Terre Verte,
Chrome Oxide Green,
Raw Umber

✧

Surfaces
Sketchbook
Prepared painting boards

✧

Size
Approximately 20 x 25 cm
(8 x 10 in)

✧

Equipment
Your outdoor painting kit
Drawing materials

✧

Time
Half an hour for each
drawing, longer for the
paintings

Sketchbook drawings allow
you to explore the natural
proportions of a subject
before committing yourself
to paint.

▼ Roadworks, market stalls
and parked cars combine in
this drawing of a country
town. This was a good
opportunity to get some bold
shapes into the foreground
as well as exploring the
longer view of the street. Use
the scale of buildings in the
background to help you
judge the scale of foreground
objects accurately.

Choose a local town as the
setting for this project. If it's
market day so much the better,
but any town will offer many
possibilities on any day of the
week. Pack the minimum
amount of gear you can into a
rucksack or paintbox, take
something to sit on and aim to
be inconspicuous.

Start by making thumbnail
sketches to try out as many
compositional possibilities as

Street Musicians, St Malo,
25.5 x 30.5 cm
(10 x 12 in).
Walking around the town I came upon this little group playing harp, guitar and dulcimer. While others listened and watched, I made a drawing. This one drawing became a whole series of drawings and colour notes and this painting was made on my return home. In an environment full of people it can be quite difficult to find situations where they remain still for long enough to provide the artist with a subject.

time allows. Make larger drawings once you've settled on a subject that you need to explore in more depth. Drawing will help you to 'break the ice' and get you working confidently in a public place. Move on to painting only when you feel completely comfortable and relaxed.

If you can position yourself away from the main tide of passers by, most people will barely notice you and you will be able to concentrate on your chosen subject. If there's no room to set up an easel, a pochade box will allow you to sit on a stool with all your painting things on your lap.

Aim to explore as many different aspects of urban life as possible and try to look beyond the obvious to find a more personal view of the subject. Some of the aspects of townscapes you might like to explore include: people in relation to buildings; people relaxing; people working; patterns of light and shadow; colour (both natural and artificial); perspective; details and textures; street furniture and clutter.

SELF-ASSESSMENT

✧ *Did you find subjects that you hadn't previously considered?*

✧ *Did you manage to capture the essence of the scene without including too many fussy details?*

✧ *Did you use your pencil as a measuring tool to check the accuracy of angles and proportions?*

CHAPTER ELEVEN

WORKING ON LOCATION

I have to admit that working on location excites me far more than painting in the relaxed atmosphere of the studio. Yes, one has to cope with changing light and uncertain weather, but there is something about decisions made at speed and under pressure that can help give a painting a sense of intensity and integrity that is difficult to achieve when one has a steady light and plenty of time. This 'now or never' attitude will enable you to paint in the most demanding conditions of changing light and movement, though you must accept that you may not be able to finish everything you start. However, the gains will more than make up for the losses. I have many paintings started in this way that were never resolved enough to put in a frame, but which nevertheless have the spark of immediate experience. Rather than discard them I use them as a sort of 'sketchbook on canvas'. Left scattered around the studio they can lift the spirits on a dull winter day, or act as a reminder to return to a particular location for another look.

▼ *Evening Walkers, West Bay,* 15 x 35.5 cm (6 x 14 in). This is my local beach and I paint here very often during the summer. The dominant horizontals of this view are countered by a spacious sky and the diminishing perspective of the walkers.

Café at Villandry,
60.5 x 50.5 cm (24 x 20 in).
Sunlight filtering through
trees, a fine building, and
people relaxing. The
Château at Villandry is world
famous for its formal gardens, but after a day
spent drawing there,
stopping for a cup of coffee
in the café gave me my
best subject.

This folding box easel is ideal for a day's painting away from home. I can carry tubes of oil colour, brushes, knife and dipper inside the box, while the sliding lid acts as a palette. It can support a canvas up to about 50cm (20in) high and the adjustable legs allow me to work either seated or standing.

TRAVELLING LIGHT

When painting on location you should reduce your equipment to the minimum and ensure that it is light and easy to carry. Struggling home at the end of the day encumbered with lots of heavy painting gear as well as two or three wet oil paintings could be a recipe for disaster! I usually take my pochade box or a folding stool and a light rucksack containing only those colours and brushes which are essential, plus some small boards, my viewfinder, a small sketchbook and pencil, small bottles of turpentine and painting medium, a palette and clip-on dipper, and a rag and some white spirit for cleaning up.

If you like to work standing up you will need a lightweight sketching easel or, even better, a combined easel and painting box in which you can carry everything, leaving one hand free for fending off stray branches or inquisitive cows. If you prefer to work sitting down, a tiny folding camping stool is easy to carry and will give you firm, if not particularly comfortable, support. A pochade box is ideal for working on location as you can work with it open on your lap and then pack everything away inside it when you've finished.

Use materials with which you are familiar. This may not be the best time to make big changes to your customary palette, or to try out an unfamiliar painting surface.

Snow in the Valley, Shipton, 10 x 22 cm (4 x 8½ in). Light snow overnight had left much of the valley green. This is one of four small panels which I painted in the course of a morning.

Sheep and Winter Weather,
15 x 20 cm (6 x 8 in).
It was a really miserable day
but these sheep with their
bright blue paint splodges
made it worthwile – even if I
did have to follow them all
over the moor!

▼ *Mirror and Comet,*
Lyme Regis,
20 x 23 cm (8 x 9 in).
By sitting with a paint box on
my lap I can paint
undisturbed as nobody takes
much notice.

TIME SCALE

A scene will look very different in the morning from later in the afternoon. As the sun tracks across the sky it can cause unexpected changes – a brilliant reflection that suddenly appears, or the wall of a house suddenly dropping into shadow, can make a big difference to a composition. These facts limit the time that you can spend painting, which in turn influences the size and scope of your work. With constantly changing light it is best to decide what it is that attracted you to the scene, then put down your impression quickly and simply before it changes. Try to see subjects that will look at their best in about an hour's time and work up to that point. Such a discipline is guaranteed to inject vitality into your paintings!

With experience and planning these things shouldn't take you by surprise too often. You'll find if you work often in a particular location you will soon get to know know how it is likely to look at a particular season or time of year. One beach that I visit regularly is lit by a low sun all through the winter, but in summer the sun sets further to the north, casting long shadows across the whole bay.

Of course, things don't always go to plan. An unexpected change in the weather, a parked lorry obstructing your selected view or a bull

occupying a previously empty field may all make you change your mind about what you're going to paint. This can be extremely frustrating. I remember once spending a long hot day painting the façade of a great house, only to return the next day to find scaffolding being put up right across 'my' view. But you can usually find alternatives, and sometimes they turn out to be less obvious and better subjects than the initial idea.

THE RIGHT SUPPORT

When you are working out of doors you need to ask yourself how much time you have, and what you can achieve in that period of time. The answers to these questions will affect the size and scope of your work. If you are painting a bustling street scene in strong sunlight you will probably spend a fair deal of time revising and restating as things move around within your composition, so working on too large a support would be impractical as it would be difficult to complete the painting in the time available. On the other hand, working very small may also slow you down and force you to draw with small movements of your fingers rather than with stronger gestures with your arm, resulting in a fussy, fiddly painting. Somewhere in between these two extremes there will be a size that suits you, but you will only discover this through trial and error.

You must also decide on format, choosing a shape for your canvas or board that ties in with your compositional idea, and avoids squeezing it into an unsuitable shape or area.

FINDING THE RIGHT SPOT

Like most landscape painters, I have certain favourite painting spots which I return to again and again. Landscape and seascape subjects are never the same twice running, so even in the most familiar territory you are unlikely to run out of subjects, and you can only gain from the intimate knowledge you develop about particular places.

On the other hand, painting somewhere new and unfamiliar can be so exciting. I used to find it difficult to get started when working in unfamiliar surroundings – there's always the lure of what might be the next corner. But I've learned from experience and now try to get painting quickly, to 'break the ice' so to speak, before spending a bit of time exploring with a sketchbook and 'getting my eye in'.

Very often when I'm out painting on location I'll notice another possible subject out of the corner of my eye. A quick note in a sketchbook will remind me to return another day and, my curiosity satisfied, I can then work on without further distraction.

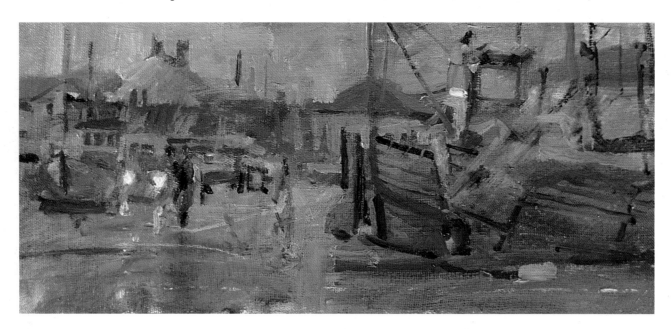

Boats on the Hard, Winter,
13 x 30 cm (5 x 12 in).
My old Land Rover makes an ideal 'hide' and provides shelter from the rain. The wet tarmac and the reflections of the car headlights provided a fascinating subject on a day when the weather was hostile.

Boadicea's Chariot,
20 x 23 cm (8 x 9 in).
I loved the amusing
juxtaposition of this heroic
statue, by Westminster Bridge
in London, with the ice-cream
van and the sightseers.

▼ *Evening Tide,*
18 x 30.5 cm (7 x 12 in).
I painted this at the end of
the day, with only a few
minutes before the light
went. It is very quickly
painted, just going for the
priorities of tone and colour.
In spite of being rather slight,
it remains one of my
favourites.

CHAPTER TWELVE

WORKING AWAY FROM A SUBJECT

There are times when it may not be convenient to carry oil-painting equipment with you, particularly if you are travelling abroad. At other times it may simply be that a marvellous subject presents itself when you are waiting for a bus or collecting the children from school, and you don't happen to have an easel, board and paints about your person. Or you may be one of those painters who find that they actually need to distance themselves from the subject, to get away from all the distractions of the landscape and distill its essence back in the studio.

For any of these reasons you might find it convenient to use another medium with which to collect useful reference material from which you can produce a painting later on. Besides, the act of drawing and sketching can be a useful filter, allowing you to clarify what excites you about a particular subject and concentrate on that aspect back in the studio. A small sketchbook and a pencil or pen can be enough to help you get the bones of the subject down and act as a spur to your visual memory.

▶ *Sunlight and Shadows in the Piazzetta San Marco*,
45.5 x 40.5 cm
(18 x 16 in)

Bob Brown,
Leon Cathedral,
charcoal,
38 x 45.5 cm
(15 x 18 in).
Compare this drawing with the painting of Chartres Cathedral by the same artist (see page 99). Notice how the selection process begins with the drawing, which enables the artist to identify what really interests him.

Bob Brown,
Detail study for *Concert at
the British Embassy, Athens*,
pencil,
27 x 38 cm (10½ x 15 in)

▼ Bob Brown,
*Study for Concert at the
British Embassy, Athens*,
watercolour and pencil,
19 x 45.5 cm (7 x 18 in)

USING REFERENCE MATERIAL

When making sketches and drawings for later use it is important to think about what sort of information you are going to need. This is where a little experience will quickly show as you begin to know what will best prompt your memory back in the studio. The sort of drawing that will be helpful is likely to contain all sorts of information about tone and colour as well as about edges and structure. It may be part drawing, part written notes, and it is very likely that several drawings, each concentrating on a different aspect of the subject, may be even more useful.

You quickly learn that there is no such thing as 'copying' the subject as each drawing, made with a different medium and a different purpose, will look quite unlike the others even though all were done together from the same viewpoint. It can be very useful to make a series of drawings from a subject, each one in a different medium and each one concentrating on a different aspect of the subject. For myself,

the way in to a new subject is often through an effect of light, so my first drawing will be a broad tonal study in ink wash or charcoal, or I might make a colour study using watercolour paints. As I'll often be trying to grasp a very transitory lighting effect, this sketch will necessarily be done very quickly. I can then follow it up with an accurate drawing in pen and ink or pencil in which I will sort out the perspective and the more linear aspects of the composition.

Although it is possible to work up a very large painting from a very small sketch it is not at all easy. Constable could work in this way and from tiny, intricate pencil drawings he produced huge canvases to send up to the Royal Academy. He had a phenomenal visual memory which helped him to do this, but he also avoided including anything very large in the

Bob Brown,
Concert at the British Embassy, Athens,
51 x 76 cm (20 x 30 in).
The sequence on these pages shows the progression from some of the drawings and colour notes which the artist made on the spot, to the finished work painted in the studio. The finished oil combines the analytical quality of the pencil drawing with the more fluid composition of the watercolour study.

foreground as on enlargement this would become overblown and out of scale with the rest of the image.

Look carefully at your drawings and decide how big a painting they will sustain. Think about the scale of the foreground, and also about whether you think the visual idea of the drawing will translate to a particular scale. Does the subject want to be intimate or expansive?

119

PROJECT
USING ON-THE-SPOT SKETCHES

✧
Medium
Oil paint
✧
Colours
Titanium White, Lemon Yellow, Cadmium Yellow, Raw Sienna, Cadmium Scarlet, Permanent Rose, French Ultramarine, Coeruleum Blue, Terre Verte, Chrome Oxide Green, Raw Umber
✧
Surfaces
Prepared painting boards
✧
Size
Approximately 20 x 25 cm (8 x 10 in)
✧
Equipment
Your outdoor painting kit
Sketchbook
Drawing materials
✧
Time
An hour for each painted sketch and two hours for a detailed drawing

My two young daughters came with me on a painting trip in France and settled down to draw in front of me. I was busy painting the view of the nearby village and didn't at first notice the girls. When I did, I quietly changed boards and made a quick oil sketch of them absorbed in their sketching. I managed to paint for about ten minutes before they noticed what I was doing. Once they'd seen me, of course, they started to pose and the naturalness of the situation was gone. I returned the following day to make a detailed drawing of the scene. Later, on my return to England, I amalgamated my studies of the scene and of the two girls to create the large finished oil shown opposite.

▲ *Village on the Loire,*
20 x 25.5 cm
(8 x 10 in)

▶ *Landscape Painters, Loire Valley,*
91.5 x 102 cm
(36 x 40 in)

◀ *Lizzie and Cal Drawing,*
20 x 25.5 cm
(8 x 10 in)

Often circumstances prevent us from making a large painting on the spot although we know the subject would work well as a big picture. Travelling away from home or working in a fickle light are just two of the reasons why it may be best to work on a small scale.

When you're next away from home, try to think hard about all the information you need to gather about your subject to enable you to build a large painting in the studio. The chances are that a pencil sketch alone won't be enough;

I often find I need a selection of painted sketches to capture the colour and atmosphere, as well as a hard-nosed piece of drawing to help put it all together when I'm miles away from the original subject and working on a bigger scale. It may be that, as in the examples on these pages, each study explores a different aspect of the view. But it will be helpful to include in addition one painting or drawing that includes everything as this will help you get the relative proportions right.

SELF-ASSESSMENT

✧ *Did you collect the right information to enable you to paint away from the subject?*

✧ *If not, what else do you consider would have been useful?*

✧ *Does your finished painting convey the freshness and immediacy of your sketches?*

CHAPTER THIRTEEN

FINISHING A PAINTING

Recognizing when a painting is finished can be quite difficult and I can clearly remember being told when I was a student to stop doing six different pictures in each painting. What the teacher meant was that I was burying the painting I had originally started under all the subsequent changes of mind and direction, and that I would have done better to actually make six separate paintings!

While it is certainly true that an underworked painting will appear superficial and slick, it is also the case that an overworked painting will be dull and lifeless. One always learns a great deal in the course of making a painting, and it is inevitable that it will shift slightly from the original concept, but there comes a point when to go any further would mean starting on a different painting, and that is the point at which to stop.

Having completed your painting, the next thing you need to consider is how it is to be presented in a way that does justice to your work.

▶ *Anemones and Mirror,*
28 x 40 cm
(11 x 16 in)

Marshwood Vale, Evening,
20 x 25.5 cm
(8 x 10 in).
Smaller paintings tend to need proportionally wider frames. The white edge around the reveal here helps to separate the painting from the frame and works better than having the gilding right up to the edge of the picture.

Varnish should be applied in a warm, dust-free room, and only when the painting is completely dry. Use a wide varnish brush and apply the varnish with long strokes, keeping the brush as flat as possible.

DEVELOPING THE PAINTING

Don't be too surprised if a painting that starts off in a promising way suddenly goes through a bit of an 'ugly duckling' phase. This will be a familiar experience to many oil painters who work in a very broad, fluid way in the initial stages. While the mental image is strongly present in your mind it is in fact easy to consider the image as a whole, and it quickly gains a feeling of unity. It is in the later stages that the danger point comes. When you start to slow down and work in more detail there is a tendency to consider the painting a section at a time and it is then that things can become rather disjointed or overworked.

Make a conscious effort to develop all areas of the canvas at the same rate so that the composition weaves itself into a whole. Keep your eye moving around the subject so that you can more easily relate areas together. Try also to see the painting as a whole by standing well back from it, or in an unfamiliar way by catching sight of it in a mirror or turning it upside down. Not only does this help you to see the image, it also highlights mistakes which may have become too familiar to notice.

VARNISHING YOUR PAINTINGS

When a painting is finished it should ideally be varnished to protect it from dust and airborne pollutants such as sulphur. Varnishing will also unify the refractive qualities of the surface of the paint and even out its appearance. If your work has gone 'patchy' (dull in some areas, shiny in others) or has 'sunk' in places (the colour has gone grey and lifeless because the oil content of the paint has been absorbed by the layers below) a layer of varnish will restore the colours to their original brilliance.

Now varnish can be a bit of a mixed blessing and many painters prefer the look of their work unvarnished. However, the modern clear synthetic varnishes are a far cry from the dark brown, sticky stuff of yesteryear, and are available in matt and gloss finishes. You can even mix the two to produce a satin finish.

You must wait at least six months for your painting to dry properly before varnishing it. However, a thin layer of retouching varnish may be applied as soon as the painting is touch-dry (that is, in about two to four weeks) and may indeed be applied between layers if necessary during the course of the painting.

FRAMING AND PRESENTATION

Oil paintings on canvas or board are usually framed without glass, but paintings on more fragile surfaces such as paper and cardboard are best framed under glass, which offers a little more protection from mechanical damage and damp.

Have your work framed as well as you can. Well doesn't necessarily mean expensively and many 'commercial' framing mouldings are much too fussy. On the whole, small paintings look best with wide, simple mouldings, while large paintings are better balanced by something relatively narrow. Plain or lightly stained timber in simple sections will often work well. Generally it is best to avoid a lot of artificial gold, though a little real gold leaf on a hand-coloured, gessoed frame can look wonderful.

Up for the Winter,
Lyme Regis,
25.5 x 30.5 cm (10 x 12 in).
One of several studies of this subject made on a cold day and used as reference for a larger picture. Carefully varnished and framed, this little study becomes a painting in its own right.

INDEX

126